The
WORST-CASE SCENARIO
Survival Handbook:
GOLF

The
WORST-CASE SCENARIO
Survival Handbook:
GOLF

By Joshua Piven, David Borgenicht, and James Grace
Illustrations by Brenda Brown

CHRONICLE BOOKS
SAN FRANCISCO

Worst-Case Scenario™ and The Worst-Case Scenario Survival Handbook™ are trademarks of Quirk Productions, Inc.

Library of Congress Cataloging-in-Publication Data available.

ISBN 0-8118-3460-3

Manufactured in Singapore

Typeset in Adobe Caslon, Bundesbahn Pi, and Zapf Dingbats

Designed by Terry Peterson
Illustrations by Brenda Brown

A **QUIRK** Book
www.quirkproductions.com
Visit www.worstcasescenarios.com

Distributed in the UK by Hi Marketing
38 Carver Road
London SE24 9LT

10 9 8 7 6 5 4 3 2 1

Chronicle Books LLC
85 Second Street
San Francisco, California 94105
www.chroniclebooks.com

WARNING

When a dire situation is at hand, safe and sane alternatives may not exist. To deal with the worst-case golfing scenarios presented in this book, we highly recommend—insist, actually—that you carefully evaluate the situation before you act; that you act responsibly and within the boundaries of the law and course rules; and that you attempt to consult a professionally trained expert, golf pro, or physician before placing yourself in harm's way. However, because highly trained professionals may not always be available when the physical or mental well-being and safety of individuals is at risk, we have asked experts on various subjects to describe the techniques they might employ in these emergency situations on and off the course. THE PUBLISHER, THE AUTHORS, AND THE EXPERTS DISCLAIM ANY LIABILITY from any harm or injury—physical or mental—that may result from the use, proper or improper, of the information contained in this book. We do not claim that the information contained herein is complete, safe, or accurate for your specific situations. Moreover, it should by no means be considered a substitute for your good judgment, skill, and common sense. And finally, nothing in this book should be construed or interpreted to infringe on the rights of other persons or entities, nor should it encourage you to violate criminal statutes or course rules: All activities described should be conducted in accordance with state and federal laws as well as the rules of the Royal and Ancient Golf Club of St. Andrews. Breaking a club is one thing—breaking the law is another.

—**The Authors**

CONTENTS

FOREWORD

My entire life has revolved around golf, in one form or another. It started when I was five. I hit my first shot on the course with my father during his regular Saturday morning game, continued playing through the collegiate and amateur ranks, and ultimately played 10 years as a touring professional. Throughout all these years, I've encountered more than my fair share of disasters on the golf course. Like all good disasters, most of these were unexpected—but ultimately they taught me quite a bit about myself and the game.

SURVIVAL RULE #1: Watch where you're driving.

One year, my friends and I decided to enter a night tournament in Phoenix. We were all good players and thought that we would win most of the prizes easily. We were in our cart approaching the green on a par-3 late in the round—it was very dark—when the cart path suddenly split. Our partners went right, we went left. The next thing I knew, I was really wet. My partner and I burst out laughing. A hundred yards away, the members of the other cart were howling, too. Sure enough, we'd driven our carts into the greenside lake—and both carts were almost completely submerged. We didn't win that tournament, but we had by far the best stories to tell at the awards party. Still, we weren't invited back.

SURVIVAL RULE #2: An eye for an eye only makes the whole tour blind.

Physical confrontations are usually few and far between on the golf course. However, early in my career I played in a Nike Tour event in Santa Rosa, California. I was paired with a friendly acquaintance for the first two rounds of the event. We had been paired together a disproportionate number of times that particular season, and I guess we were just growing a little tired of each other.

After he brought it home in 42 on the back nine to ruin a front nine 31, he signed his scorecard, approached me, and proceeded to antagonistically inform me that the lack of heart, talent, skill, and character he displayed on the back nine were all my fault. (In truth, some of it probably was, because I wasn't playing very inspired golf after a horrible front nine that left my clubs and my enthusiasm bruised and battered.)

Not wanting to get fined or suspended by decking him right then and there, I calmly listened to him and politely disagreed with everything he said. I tried chalking it up to end-of-the-year weariness, but it festered in my mind all night, and I knew that the next day would be agonizing, because we were still paired together. So I decided something had to be done.

On the driving range in the morning, I dropped my clubs, went over to him, and said, "If you have any intention of talking to me in that tone again, be prepared to settle it like a man." I spent the rest of the day trying to antagonize him into starting a physical confrontation.

In the end, we both played horribly, we both acted like children, and we both knew that our emotions cost us any chance of performing well in that tournament. To this day we're still friends, but I hope I never have to play golf with him again.

SURVIVAL RULE #3: When the weather gets rough, get going.

During the first round of the 1991 US Open, I was on the golf course putting out on the sixth green as a storm produced some vicious lightning. In those days, we were still allowed to complete the hole we were playing even if play was suspended due to threatening weather—and we decided to do so. Once finished, we were herded into a school bus, and we heard the sirens of an ambulance. We later learned that a spectator was killed by a bolt of lightning. Later that same year, another spectator was killed at the PGA Championship in Indianapolis. The danger of lightning was now thoroughly understood by everyone in golf.

Later in my career, I was among a group of three that actually terminated play for the entire field at a Nike Tour event in Shreveport, Louisiana. We felt in danger because of lightning, and decided to walk off the course. Our decision wasn't overly popular with the rules officials, but we weren't about to take any chances. You shouldn't either.

Golf has taught me many valuable lessons, and it has brought me many joys—but I still never know what's awaiting me on the next hole. Expect the unexpected. And the next time you find yourself in a situation that you never dreamed possible, remember, I warned you.

—Jerry Foltz, Tournament Player and Journalist

When I'm on a golf course and it starts to
rain and lightning, I hold up my one iron,
'cause I know even God can't hit a one iron.
—Lee Trevino

They say that life is a lot like golf—don't believe them.
Golf is a lot more complicated.
—Gardner Dickinson

INTRODUCTION

A triple bogey is the least of your problems!

Even if you think your game is under control and you are spending most of your time on the fairway and greens, you're at risk—the most dangerous sort of risk, because you think you are safe. But a round of golf can turn to nightmare in seconds: a bird suddenly attacks; a cart careens out of control; an alligator claims your ball. Even if you never have to disarm an angry golfer or extinguish a cigar brush fire—never need to stick your hand down a gopher hole, never hit a beehive, and never attempt to scale a fence to retrieve a wayward ball—you may face great peril on the links.

Many of these dangers are physical: every year, one out of two golfers is injured during play. To be sure, most of these injuries are not life-threatening—but the odds of walking off the last green unscathed are about as good as a coin flip. Even worse, think about this fact: you are more likely to get hit by lightning during the round than to hit an absolutely perfect drive off the first tee. (Lee Trevino, the celebrated touring professional, has been hit by lightning twice.) And every year, countless golfers are hit by golf balls traveling up to 130 miles per hour. With more than 100 million golfers around the world each hitting an average of 100 shots per round (97 for men, 114 for women, according to the National Golf Foundation), it's a wonder more of us haven't been hit.

Other perils are mental: you might worry about what club to use or which way the green breaks, but the really dangerous thing to worry about is worry itself. If you spend your time on and off the course worrying about your slice or your hook, becoming more and more aggravated over that bad shot and more and more obsessed with your game, you may hurt not only your playing, but your loved ones and livelihood as well—for these are the early signs of a golf addiction.

Even if you manage to avoid the physical and psychological dangers of the game, the rules of golf alone can ensnare you, costing you a match, a tournament, or even worse, a bet.

So we want you to be prepared for the worst golf has in store, no matter what the source.

As in our earlier *Worst-Case Scenario Survival Handbooks*, we have consulted a battalion of experts to help you survive the game, this time including golf pros, doctors, meteorologists, self-defense instructors, zoologists, and professional gamblers. The scenarios in this handbook are arranged into four chapters: playing out of difficult situations, dealing with equipment malfunctions, fending off dangerous creatures, and surviving a variety of other golf crises. We have also explained, throughout the book as well as in the appendix, how the official rules of golf apply to what you might encounter on the course, whether dangerous or just bizarre. The appendix also provides a handy glossary of golf slang, information on an assortment of fashion emergencies, and a guide to some of the more popular ways to wager on the golf course, should you feel lucky.

This book may not help you improve your swing, but it just might keep you physically and mentally healthy enough to come back and play another day. Because you just never know what you will encounter between the tee and the green.

So keep your head down, take a deep breath, and carry this book in your cart or bag. (Or keep it next to you on the couch when you watch golf on TV.)

Forewarned is forearmed.

—The Authors

Chapter 1

BAD LIES

HOW TO RETRIEVE A BALL LOST IN THE WASHER

There are two common types of ball washers. One has a vertical, central cylinder in which the ball is placed. This cylinder slides up and down on a rod surrounded by brushes and soapy water. The other common type of washer has a circular cylinder and a crank; the ball makes several rotations through brushes or a rubber squeegee and soapy water with one crank.

VERTICAL BALL WASHER

1 Use a stick or shoehorn to dislodge the ball.
If the portion of the washer that slides up and down breaks off, the ball and cylinder may come to rest in the bottom of the bucket, out of reach of your fingers.

2 Attempt to scoop the ball out of the broken cylinder.

3 Use a screwdriver to disassemble the washer.
If you are unable to pry the ball out, take apart the washer. If a screwdriver is not available, use a metal cleat tightener.

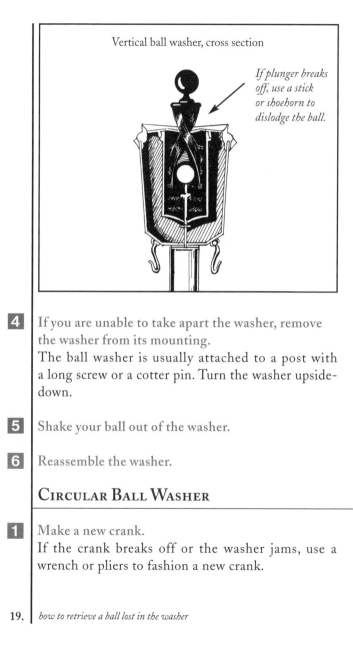

Vertical ball washer, cross section

If plunger breaks off, use a stick or shoehorn to dislodge the ball.

4 | If you are unable to take apart the washer, remove the washer from its mounting.
The ball washer is usually attached to a post with a long screw or a cotter pin. Turn the washer upside-down.

5 | Shake your ball out of the washer.

6 | Reassemble the washer.

CIRCULAR BALL WASHER

1 | Make a new crank.
If the crank breaks off or the washer jams, use a wrench or pliers to fashion a new crank.

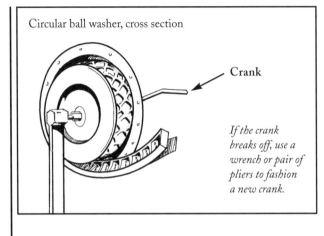

Circular ball washer, cross section

Crank

If the crank breaks off, use a wrench or pair of pliers to fashion a new crank.

2 | Take apart the washer.
If the improvised crank does not work, disassemble the washer (see steps 3 through 6, previous page).

Be Aware
- Greens keepers frown upon tampering with golf equipment. It may be better to simply use a new ball.
- Golf etiquette dictates that you should not delay play. If you think it will require more than a few minutes to disassemble the ball washer, retrieve your ball, and reassemble the washer, keep moving instead.

The Rule
No penalty is assessed for a ball lost in the washer.

HOW TO TEE OFF IN FRONT OF A CROWD

1 Relax.

Try to see the first tee as any other shot in the round. Do not make significant changes in your tempo. Try not to rush any aspect of your pre-shot routine or swing. Ignore comments from the crowd waiting to play, or pressure from the starter to speed up.

2 Warm up.

Thoroughly stretch in whatever way increases blood flow to your body and feels good. Take as many practice swings as you need.

Focus your thoughts on your mind, body, and swing.

3 | Release the tension in your body.
Identify where the tension is, consciously tighten that area of your body, and then consciously relax that area while noticing the difference. Take a deep breath—in through your nose and out through your mouth—before you hit.

4 | Be mindful.
Tune in to your feelings prior to your first swing. Are you nervous? Anxious? Steeped in self-judgment? Be aware of these negative feelings and the consequences of them on your body. Recognize that these feelings often get in the way of your true golf swing and game. Replace those feelings with positive energy. Choose to feel competent and content. Remember a time when you played your best. Generate these thoughts until you are ready to hit the ball.

5 | Be confident about your abilities and expectations.
If you hit the ball 200 yards 80 percent of the time, you will most likely hit the ball 200 yards this time. This does not mean that you should not strive for your personal best throughout the game. Recognize that the first tee is a starting point on which you are building a solid foundation for your day's golf game.

6 | Select the club with which you feel most comfortable.
This may not be your driver. Use a long iron or three wood if your driver is not your best club off the tee.

7 Follow a routine for addressing the ball.
Keep to an established pattern of how you walk up
to the tee, how many practice swings you take, how
you set your stance, and at what moment you start
your swing. This routine is especially important on
the first tee.

8 Do not overanalyze your swing.
Your muscle memory will complete the swing for you
if you cease to over-think it. Do not over-swing in an
effort to hit the ball farther.

9 Focus.
Choose a single location on the fairway and aim at
that spot.

Be Aware

• Spend time on the practice tee prior to hitting off
the first tee. Go through six to eight clubs in your
bag—start with wedges (they are easy to swing) and
work your way up to woods. Visualize hitting off
the first tee on your last 10 to 12 practice drives.

• Golf is the culmination of physical, emotional, and
mental preparedness. It is a game that begins and
ends in both the body and the mind of the golfer.
The first tee is the initial setting where you need
to understand and accept the interrelation of
these three elements.

HOW TO RETRIEVE A BALL STUCK IN A TREE

If your ball is lodged in a tree, you have the option to play it as it lies or declare it unplayable. No matter which decision you make, you will need to climb the tree to access the ball.

1 Attempt to identify the ball from the ground.
The rules require that a player identify his or her ball prior to hitting or moving it. You will save yourself a climb if you can determine from the ground that the ball is not yours.

2 Determine if the tree is dead or alive.
Do not climb dead trees—they are much more dangerous than living trees. A dead tree's limbs may break unexpectedly.

3 Survey the tree and surrounding area for hazards.
Do not climb a tree that is touching or is intertwined with power lines. Look into the tree to determine if there are any animal nests near your ball. Although most animals will flee when you get close, squirrels protecting their nests and raccoons living in the hollow of a tree may be dangerous.

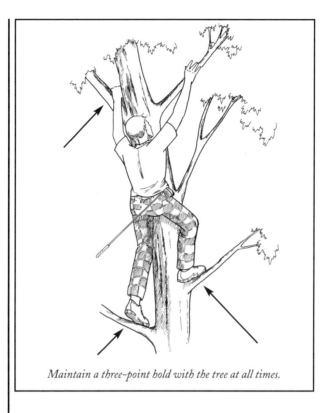

Maintain a three-point hold with the tree at all times.

4 Grab a branch at its base or "crotch."

The strongest and thickest part of the branch is the place it splits from the trunk. The farther you go out on the branch, the weaker it is. Be careful not to grab a dead branch.

5 Use your legs, not your arms, to power yourself up the tree.

Your arms should only guide your ascent.

6 Maintain a three-point hold when you are in the tree.

Make sure that three parts of your body are attached to or touching the tree at all times; for example, if both feet are on the trunk, have at least one hand on a branch above as you reach to go farther.

7 If you need to rest, wrap your arms around the tree or a sturdy branch.

Try to use your legs to support you, if possible, rather than your arms.

8 Reach out to your ball.

Either knock it to the ground or put it in your pocket.

9 Begin your descent.

Your arms should bear your weight on the way down. To increase your grip on the branches during your descent, turn your palms toward you when gripping the branches.

10 Follow the same path to go down as you took when you went up.

Be Aware

• Buds or leaves on a tree indicate that it is living. Although the tree as a whole may be alive, you still need to watch for dead branches. Dead branches may be discolored compared to the rest of the tree and they may be missing their bark.

- Do not climb a tree if you are alone. If you encounter problems, your partner might be able to assist you or find someone who can.
- Cover your eyes with glasses or sunglasses prior to climbing, if possible. Twigs and branches may poke you. Wear a hardhat or baseball cap to help protect your head.
- Do not climb a tree when it is raining or if the tree is wet. The tree will be slippery.

The Rules

If you shake the tree to get the ball down for the purpose of identifying it (before declaring it unplayable), you will incur a two-stroke penalty.

If, before declaring your ball unplayable, you swing at a branch lower than where your ball sits and you move the ball, you have incurred a one-stroke penalty for moving your ball. You must replace the ball. You are not charged a stroke for the swing at the branch. If you cannot replace the ball, you must now declare the ball unplayable and add a stroke to your score.

how to retrieve a ball stuck in a tree

HOW TO RETRIEVE A BALL FROM A GOPHER HOLE

1 Determine whether your ball is in a gopher hole.
If you were able to see your ball land and you have checked that area carefully, look for a gopher hole. A gopher hole will be a well-groomed hole in the ground approximately two to three inches in diameter. There may be a cluster of gopher holes, especially if you are in the rough near the edge of the woods.

2 Attempt to make visual contact with the ball.
Do not put your hand down the hole. You do not know what is down there.

3 If you see the ball, use your longest club to hook the ball and drag it toward the top of the hole.
Use your two or three iron, a long club with a relatively small club head. A ball retriever, designed for water hazards, may also work.

4 Pick up the ball with your other hand as it comes close to the top of the hole.

5 Leave the area quickly.
The animal you have disturbed may be angered by your invasion. While most animals are more afraid of you than you are of them, caution is always the best policy.

chapter 1: bad lies

Be Aware

- A ball in the depths of a gopher hole is nearly impossible to see. Be sure to keep your eye on the ball if there are gopher holes on the course. Use at least two points of reference to mark where your ball lands.
- The gopher's burrow system may be linear or highly branched. A single burrow system may be up to 200 yards long. Underground tunnels are two to three inches in diameter and usually are 6 to 12 inches below the ground, but they may be more than six feet deep. You may need to use a flashlight to see within the complex maze.
- Gophers have menacing upper and lower teeth that are always exposed. They also have strong forepaws with large claws. If you are bitten or clawed, seek medical attention immediately. Although gophers are normally shy, they will bite.

The Rules

Once you identify your ball, you must advise your fellow players that you will be lifting it. You can pick up your ball without a penalty and drop it at the nearest point of relief from where it lies. If you are not in a hazard, the nearest point of relief is one club length from the nearest location no closer to the hole that allows you to take your normal stance and swing. If you are in a hazard, you cannot remove the ball without taking a penalty stroke.

how to retrieve a ball from a gopher hole

If the ball is lost in the gopher hole, you may replace it without penalty. This is an exception to the general rule that a lost ball will cost you a stroke. The main question your opponents will have is whether there is reasonable evidence that your ball disappeared into a gopher hole rather than that the ball was lost elsewhere.

HOW TO SCALE A FENCE TO RETRIEVE A BALL

1 | Look for a gate.
If you cannot reach over, under, or through a fence to retrieve your ball, you will need to get to the other side. A nearby unlocked gate is the easiest means. If the gate is locked, the lock mechanism may serve as a good foothold.

2 | Look for the best part of the fence to scale.
Assess the fence for hand- and footholds. Typically, fences will be either chain-link or slatted wood. Chain-link fences, the more common type, provide excellent hand- and footholds. If the fence is wood, look for a part of the fence with a support post (preferably on both sides).

3 | Assess the dangers of your landing area.
If the ground on the other side of the fence slopes off, make sure you can see what is at the bottom of the slope. Look also for rocks, soft sand, thorns, mud, water, or other hazards that may jeopardize your safety during and after your landing. Look for signs of animals. Snakes, alligators, or guard dogs may lurk on the other side. Whistle, or shake the fence before you attempt to climb; an animal may reveal itself.

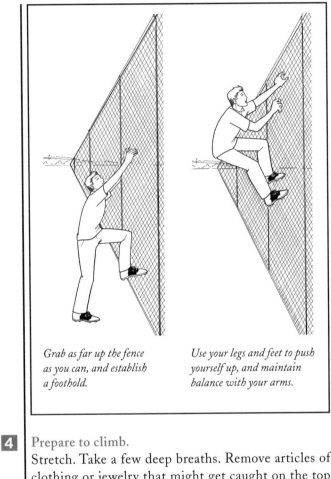

Grab as far up the fence as you can, and establish a foothold.

Use your legs and feet to push yourself up, and maintain balance with your arms.

4 Prepare to climb.

Stretch. Take a few deep breaths. Remove articles of clothing or jewelry that might get caught on the top of the fence.

5 Grab the fence as high as you can reach.

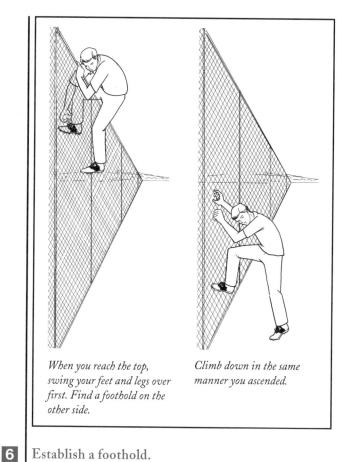

When you reach the top, swing your feet and legs over first. Find a foothold on the other side.

Climb down in the same manner you ascended.

6 Establish a foothold.

Try to get as much of your toe on the foothold (or inside it) without getting it wedged too tightly. Use the cleats in your golf shoes to clip onto the fence.

7 Use your legs and feet to push yourself up.
Maintain balance with your arms, and pull as needed.
Your leg muscles are bigger and stronger than those in
your arms. Your arms will tire more quickly, which may
affect your ability to get back over the fence.

8 When you reach the top, determine the best method
for your descent.
You may be able to climb down the fence in the same
manner you ascended: place your feet over the fence
first, finding a foothold that will support you as you
lower yourself with your arms.

Or

Go over headfirst.
Place your stomach on top of the fence, dip your head
down, and swing your legs over and down. If the top of
the fence is sharp or jagged, do not use this method.

Or

Jump.
Golf shoes will not absorb the impact of a jump of any
significant distance. Aim for a clear landing spot,
deeply bend your knees on landing, and be prepared to
roll. Roll to your strong side (i.e., if you are right-
handed, roll to your right). Tuck your shoulder and
continue to let yourself roll until you come to a stop
naturally.

9 Retrieve your ball.

Place it in your pocket or toss it over the fence. Do not hold it in your hand as you climb back over.

10 Repeat the process to return to the course side of the fence.

Be Aware

• A ball retriever can help you reach a ball lying just on the other side of the fence. If you do not carry a specially designed ball retriever, be cautious about reaching through a fence with a club: you could wind up losing the club as well as the ball.

• Do not trespass. Although people living along a golf course may be used to people invading their land, trespassing is a crime, and a serious fence may be an indication that the owner will protect property rights.

The Rule

Hitting a ball out of bounds incurs a one-stroke penalty. The rule also states that you must hit your next shot from where you originally played the ball, not from where it landed. If you play your ball from its out of bounds position, you will be assessed a two-stroke penalty in stroke play and a loss-of-hole penalty in match play.

how to scale a fence to retrieve a ball

HOW TO PLAY OUT OF A WATER TRAP

1 Determine what is under your ball.
Ascertain what is beneath the water and whether you are hitting off sand or a rock bed before you take the shot. Unknowingly swinging into a hard surface can do significant damage to your hands or wrists and your club.

2 Calculate the ball's depth.
The more of the ball that is showing above the water line, the better. The reliability of executing this shot decreases considerably if the top of the ball is more than half an inch below the water line.

3 Take off your shoes and socks.
If you cannot stand on the bank, step into the water barefoot.

Try to determine what is underneath your ball before you swing. Unknowingly hitting a hard surface may damage your hands, wrists, or club.

Open the club face slightly. Aim behind the ball, swing down and through it.

4 Wear a raincoat or other foul-weather gear.
There will be a large spray that may include mud.

5 Grip the club firmly.
Because the club will be moving through something with a high resistance—water—the club head will twist if you do not maintain a firm hold.

6 Open the club head slightly.
The club head will naturally close as the club moves through the water.

7 Aim behind the ball.
Play the shot as if the ball were buried in the sand. Hit the water approximately one ball length behind the ball. Do not be concerned about refraction of the light through the water; the ball is not deep enough for this to be a factor.

8 Swing down and through the ball.
Hit the ball hard. It will be the force of the water behind the ball that carries the ball out, not the impact with the club face itself.

Be Aware
- Going into or near the water may not be a good idea due to the possible presence of snakes, alligators, and other animals, particularly in natural water hazards. Courses along the ocean or deep lakes pose issues of general water safety. Check for posted signs throughout the course that warn of local hazards or dangerous animals.
- Check the back of the scorecard for local rules that might apply to hitting out of the water.

The Rule
Your club cannot make contact with the water in the hazard prior to your shot. If contact is made, a two-stroke penalty will be assessed or in match play you will lose the hole.

HOW TO PLAY OUT OF HIGH SAW GRASS

Saw grass is a large plant (between four and ten feet tall) with flat, stiff, narrow leaf blades that have small, sharp sawteeth along the midribs. Often, dense saw grass will be out-of-bounds or in a hazard, but under some circumstances you may be able to play a ball that is nestled in saw grass.

1 Determine if you are in a hazard.
Look for hazard markers. The rules are stricter when hitting out of a hazard.

2 Prepare to enter the grass.
Wear gloves on both of your hands to avoid getting cut. Be sure to wear long pants to protect your legs. Spray any exposed areas on your arms and legs with bug repellent to avoid contact with insects (e.g., ticks, chiggers, etc.).

3 Identify your ball.
Use your index finder and thumb to pick up the ball. Mark the location of the ball, turn the ball over to see the markings, and then place it back in the exact same position. Do not clean your ball when identifying it. If you are in a hazard, you must first hit the ball and then identify it. If it is not in fact your ball, there is no penalty, but you must return to the grass to find your ball (and return the ball you hit to the spot you found it).

4 Use a wedge.

The heavy bottom of a sand wedge or pitching wedge will help the club head slice through the grass. Its open face will increase loft, so that the ball will land softly. Never hit a wood out of high grass.

5 Take a practice swing.

Find a spot away from the ball that has a similar rough and lie. Get a feel for how the club will react to plowing through the grass.

6 Set up the club level with the ball.

Since the ball may be propped up several inches above the ground, be careful not to align the club underneath the ball. In order to make up the distance that the higher grass has created, choke up on the club.

7 Stand so that the ball is forward of the center of your stance.

Play the ball between your front ankle and the center of your stance.

8 Open your stance and the club face slightly.

Take your club back in a V-shaped swing rather than a U-shaped swing. Do this by cocking your wrists more quickly as you take the club away from the ball.

9   If you are a right-handed golfer, the ball will have a tendency to go to the left.

To prevent this, grip the club firmly with your left hand and normally with your right hand. If you are left-handed, grip the club firmly with your right hand and normally with your left. Also, open the club face to decrease the likelihood of it closing as it fights its way through the grass prior to impact. Open the face to between 25 and 30 degrees.

10   Accelerate the club head through the ball.

Use the weight of the club and the added wrist cock to increase the club head speed down through impact.

11   Shift the weight in your lower body as you hit.

Adding a more pronounced weight shift will help you develop enough speed on your club head to pop the ball out of the grass.

The Rules

A two-stroke penalty will be assessed if you use your hands, club, or feet to improve the lie around the ball. Matting down the grass around the ball is prohibited.

When you sole your club at address, you may inadvertently create an indentation in the grass into which your ball may roll. This incurs a one-stroke penalty. If the ball is in a hazard, the rules do not permit you to ground your club at all.

HOW TO CAROM
THE BALL OFF
A WALL

If your ball lands within a few feet of a wall, you may need to carom the ball off the wall. The ball's proximity to the wall may make it impossible for you to make a proper stroke.

1 Choose a club with enough loft to get the ball as high as possible off the wall.
Choose a club that has the loft of a seven iron or greater. A nine iron or pitching wedge is the most common choice. The higher on the wall that the ball hits, the farther it will travel.

2 Aim for the smoothest spot on the wall.
The direction of the shot will be greatly affected by the surface of the wall. The smoother the wall, the more predictable the shot will be.

3 If possible, play the ball in the middle of your stance.
This is the ideal stance for this shot. However, if you are only a few ball lengths from the wall, you will have no choice but to play the ball closer to your front foot. The closeness to the wall may have the greatest effect on the extent of your follow-through.

Hit a punch shot and aim for the smoothest spot on the wall.

4 Map out the ricochet.
The ball will bounce off the wall at the same angle that it hits. Decide where you want the ball to land and imagine a line extending to that spot from the wall. Pick the spot on the wall for which the angle coming off the wall is equal to the angle toward the wall, and mark the spot in your mind. This is much like a bank shot in billiards.

5 Hit a "punch shot" to limit the follow-through.
Keep your hands in front of the ball and take the club away vertically by cocking your wrists. Hit down into the ball and then into the ground under the ball in order to create enough force to get the ball off the wall with as little follow-through as possible. Imagine you are swinging an ax.

The Rules

You cannot push, scrape, or spoon the ball to gain better positioning or you will incur a two-stroke penalty. You must play the ball as it lies.

If the ball comes off the wall and hits your body, equipment, or caddie, you will be assessed a two-stroke penalty. You will have to play the ball where it lies. Move your equipment and caddie away from the shot and keep your body out of the line of the shot as much as possible. If your body is in the line of the shot, it may be better to declare the ball unplayable and take a one-stroke penalty, but make certain that your lie for the next shot improves.

Some walls on golf courses may be considered an "immovable obstruction" from which relief is available. Local rules would apply.

HOW TO THWART A CHEAT

Cheating at golf is so pervasive it seems to be part of the game: even people playing alone do it. There are mulligans off the tee, gimmies on the green, and lots of ways to get an unfair advantage in between. Here are a few of the most common scams and how to recognize and defeat them.

THE LOST BALL ROUTINE

While searching for a ball lost in the woods, the player drops another ball that he has been carrying and falsely announces to the group that he has found his original ball. He has saved himself a penalty stroke and has positioned the ball as he pleases. A variation on this play is to find a stray ball, claim it, hit it, and move on quickly.

Always keep an eye on your opponent.

1 Make a mental note of the markings on your opponent's ball at the start of the round.
Notice color, scratches, brand, and number.

2 Always help to look for a missing ball, and keep an eye on your opponent as well.
Two people searching also speeds up play.

IMPROVING A LIE

The cheat gently taps her ball with a foot or the club, gaining a more favorable position.

1 Stand near your opponent so that you can see the ball at all times.

2 Always watch your opponent, and, more important, let her know that she is being watched at all times.
Subtle comments about her technique, her attire, or the nuances of her address will let her know she's being carefully observed. You do not have to stand by her side all day long, but put yourself in a position where you can see any errant moves. Being under constant surveillance makes most people less inclined to bend the rules.

3 Note how much of the ball is visible as you approach it, and mark its position in relation to nearby objects, such as roads, trees, and traps.
As the cheat goes to take the shot, the amount of the ball that is visible to you, even at a distance, should not change. Watch also for substantial changes in the ball's location; some players do not stop at simply tapping the ball to improve the lie.

Reporting Fewer Strokes

On a hole on which everything went wrong, she drops a few strokes from the score before announcing or recording it. She realizes that most opponents will lose track at around eight or nine strokes, and may not question such a total for fear of embarrassing themselves or the player.

1 Keep score carefully yourself.
See "How to Keep Score without a Pencil" on page 69.

2 Ask for a careful account of each stroke after every hole.
Be supportive of your golfing companion. When she has a difficult hole, tell her to hang in there, that it happens to the best, and so on—but when the hole is complete, ask her to recap the hole in a friendly, sympathetic manner.

Playing Dumb

Though he has hit his ball out of bounds, into the water, or in any other situation where penalty strokes are applicable, he tries to take only one penalty stroke where two are warranted.

1 At the completion of the hole, ask for a clear account of the score and applicable penalty strokes.

2 If there is any debate, be courteous, but firm.
If the scoring remains unresolved, take it up with
the club pro at the end of the round.

FAKE HANDICAP

Someone who has a five handicap introduces himself
to a group of strangers and announces a higher handicap. After shooting a 78, he claims that it was the
round of his life, and is somewhat sheepish about
taking everyone's money.

1 Take out your own USGA handicap card as you are
having the discussion about handicaps.
Tell the stranger that you have all agreed to show each
other your cards before starting.

2 At the end of nine holes, assess where this individual stands.
If it is clear that things are not what they appear,
demand an adjustment in his stated handicap. If he
balks, play the back nine, but state that the competition or bet is off. If someone you just met dumps
the front nine, scoring above his alleged handicap, be
cautious about increasing ("pressing") a bet on the
back nine. It could be a setup.

Be Aware
• Keeping an opponent honest requires you to be
  observant and to hold everyone accountable for his
  or her strokes as the round unfolds. This may seem

tedious at times, and may cause some odd interactions with your opponents. You must decide
what is more important to you: interpersonal
relations or winning.

- Cheating can occur even when there is no betting
or competition between players. A player seeking
to claim a new course record or his own personal
best score can seek to shave strokes from the scorecard. You can decide how involved you want to be.

HOW TO STOP THINKING ABOUT A HORRIBLE SHOT

1 Express your displeasure.

It is important to express your anger or frustration with your bad shot so that you can let it go—just be sure to do so responsibly. Vent in a tactful way, in a manner that will not do damage to the golf course, your equipment, or another player.

2 Praise yourself for what you did right—and for the good shots you have had.

It is important to recognize your abilities. Pat yourself on the back. Do not get carried away, however; too much self-praise can lead to overconfidence.

3 Try to relax.

Breathe from the abdomen, in through the nose and out through the mouth.

4 Accept the fact that you will hit a few bad shots in any round.

If you know—but do not fixate on the fact—that you will hit a few bad shots during your round, your anticipation will replace your frustration. Create a checklist in your mind that includes potentially good and bad drives, approach shots, and putts. When you make one of your bad shots, simply check it off of your list and be glad it is gone.

5 Know that you cannot change the past, you can only alter the future.
There is no point in looking back to what was because there is nothing you can do about it.

6 Concentrate on your shots one at a time.
Each shot requires your focused attention based on the factors that are present at that moment.

7 Find your zone.
Learn to find that place where you feel empty just before you swing the club and let your shot happen.

8 Hit your next shot with confidence.

EQUIPMENT DISASTERS

HOW TO STOP A RUNAWAY CART

IF YOU ARE IN THE CART

1 Attempt to shut off the cart.
If the cart is electric, turn the ignition key to the "off" position. If the cart is gas powered, do not turn the key to the "off" position—leave it in gear.

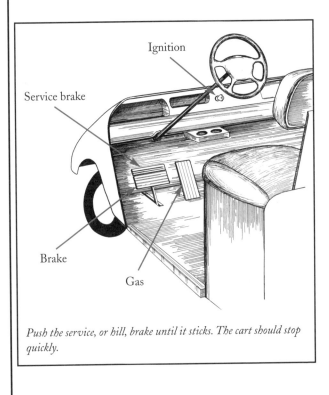

Push the service, or hill, brake until it sticks. The cart should stop quickly.

2 Try to engage the service brake.

The service, or hill, brake is located on the top half of the brake pedal. Push it forward until it sticks. If it engages, the cart should stop quickly.

3 If the service brake fails, wait for the automatic emergency system to stop the cart.

If you are still moving, there has been a brake failure. Most late-model electric carts also have "downhill braking," an automatic emergency system that is designed to stop the cart in the event of downhill acceleration. This emergency brake should now engage. Gas carts do not use downhill braking: They have compression braking, which uses the engine to stop the cart experiencing uncontrolled acceleration. This emergency system should also activate automatically.

4 If the cart does not stop, attempt to ride it out.

You should be able to steer a golf cart even with the key turned off. Stay in the cart and steer onto a gentle incline, which will slow or stop it. Do not jerk the wheel or make any sharp turns. If the car is accelerating downhill or into unsafe terrain and you cannot slow it down, prepare to exit.

5 Jump out of the cart.

Do not try to land on your feet. Leap out and away from the path of the cart, rolling on your side to lessen the impact until you are at a safe distance. Protect your head with your arms and aim for grass or other forgiving terrain.

Leap out and away from the path of the cart, rolling onto your shoulder. Do not try to land on your feet.

If You Are Not in the Cart

1 Evaluate the situation.

If an empty cart is accelerating downhill and you are far behind, you may not be able to reach it. If the cart is headed uphill or into scrub brush rather than a water hazard, and there are no people in front of the cart, it may slow down on its own. If the cart is headed toward people, a green, or another area where it may cause damage, you may be able to intercept it.

2 Chase the cart and match its speed.

Unless the cart is traveling in a straight line downhill from your position, run at an angle that will allow you to catch up with it.

3 Grab the roof or a roof support.

If the cart is a model without a roof, grab the back of the seat. Do not reach for the wheel before you are in the cart, or you risk turning the cart into your path and running yourself over.

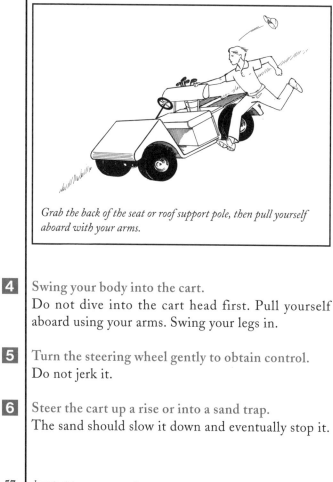

Grab the back of the seat or roof support pole, then pull yourself aboard with your arms.

4 Swing your body into the cart.

Do not dive into the cart head first. Pull yourself aboard using your arms. Swing your legs in.

5 Turn the steering wheel gently to obtain control.

Do not jerk it.

6 Steer the cart up a rise or into a sand trap.

The sand should slow it down and eventually stop it.

Be Aware

• The industry maximum speed for both electric and gas golf carts is about 14 miles per hour. (Special vehicles can reach speeds of 18 mph.) A runaway golf cart is usually traveling only with momentum, not with electric or gas power, and should not be traveling at more than a few miles per hour, unless it is going down a hill.

• Always set the hill brake when leaving the cart, whether or not you have stopped on a hill.

Failure to set the brake can lead to a runaway cart (see page 60 for towing instructions).

HOW TO GET A CART OUT OF A SAND TRAP

1 Check that the rear wheels are on the ground.

All golf carts are rear-wheel drive and carts have very little chassis ground clearance; they can easily get stuck on uneven terrain. If the cart is partially in, partially out of a trap, or if the trap is on a slope, make sure the rear wheels are on the ground.

Create traction by piling sand, rocks, sticks, and clothing under the wheel in the trap.

2 Attempt to push the cart onto the ground to obtain more traction.

The average cart weighs about 800 pounds, but two or three players should be able to push it forward or back enough so that the rear wheels will grab.

3 If you cannot get it onto solid ground, create traction.

The tire treads on golf carts are very shallow and will not provide much traction. Try piling sand or small stones around the wheel to increase traction, or place jackets and other clothing under the rear wheels. An empty, collapsible golf bag may also work.

4 Flag down a passing cart and ask for a tow.

5 Tow the cart.

Secure a long, sturdy rope or chain to a tow hook on the chassis in the rear of the cart. If no hook is available, secure the rope or chain to the chassis using several good knots. Secure the other end of the rope to the rear of another cart, on the chassis. A single golf cart should be powerful enough to pull a disabled cart out of trouble. Use slow, steady acceleration to tow the cart until it has become dislodged and can be driven. If no other cart is available, three to five people may be necessary to push or pull the cart out.

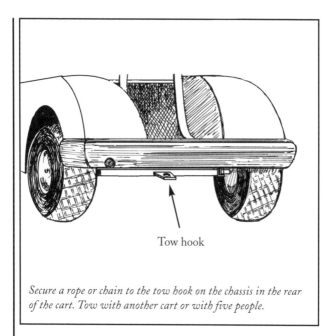

Tow hook

Secure a rope or chain to the tow hook on the chassis in the rear of the cart. Tow with another cart or with five people.

Be Aware

- Golf carts use an open differential drive train: the power will go to the rear wheel that has the most traction.

- If the cart is stuck in a bunker on a hill, use caution when towing or driving out. If the hill is steep, do not attempt to drive the cart in a direction that is parallel to the slope of the terrain; you risk losing traction and slipping or possibly overturning. Golf carts are not designed to be used on hills with more than a 25-percent grade (14-degree slope). Be especially careful on wet grass.

HOW TO START A
DEAD CART

1 Move the key switch to the "off" position.
If you do not have the key, borrow one from another cart; most cart keys are interchangeable.

2 Locate the battery.
The vast majority of golf-cart power failures are due to problems with the battery connections. The battery (or batteries) is generally located under the driver's seat.

3 Cover your eyes.
Put on glasses, sunglasses, or protective goggles before touching the battery.

4 Move the tow/maintenance switch to "off."
Most electric carts have a towing switch that provides power to the electric speed controller. Turning it off will help to prevent arcing (sparking) across the battery. The tow/maintenance switch should be located near the battery. Note that instead of "on" and "off," the switch may be labeled "run" and "tow/maintenance," respectively.

5 Check the terminals for corrosion.
Look for corrosion where the wires meet the battery terminals. A poor connection at one of the battery terminals may cause the cart to stop running.

6 Secure the connection.

A loose connection can cause the amperage to increase, which can damage the cart's electrical system and prevent it from running. Use clamp-on pliers or vise grips to secure the wire-to-terminal connection. Wear your golfing glove(s) for safety.

7 Move the tow maintenance switch to "on" (or "run").

8 Move the key switch to the "on" position to start the cart.

9 Put the cart in gear, depress the accelerator, and drive.

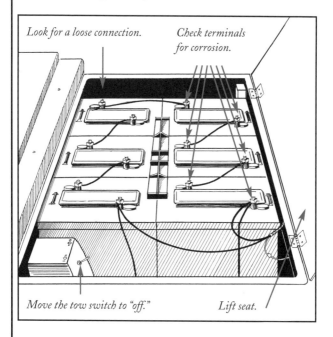

Look for a loose connection.

Check terminals for corrosion.

Move the tow switch to "off."

Lift seat.

Starting Dead Gas Carts

- Starter problems with gas carts are usually battery related. First check the battery connections. Repair as appropriate (see preceeding pages).

- Check to see if you have run out of gas. Refill the tank if it is empty.

- Check the fuel lines and filter for a blockage or faulty connection. If the problem is not apparent, abandon the cart.

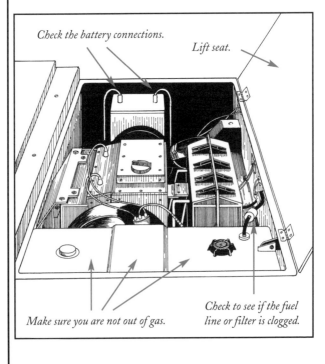

Check the battery connections.

Lift seat.

Make sure you are not out of gas.

Check to see if the fuel line or filter is clogged.

HOW TO PUTT
WITH A DRIVER

1 Choke up on the grip.
A driver is longer than most putters. For comfort and control, place your hands lower than you do when you are using the club to drive.

2 Keep your feet relatively close together.
Stand taller than you normally do, playing the ball in a position opposite your forward foot.

Position your eyes over the target line.

Choke up on the grip.

Slant the club forward.

Hit the ball low on the face.

Stand with your feet close together.

3 Move your hands in very close to your body and slant the club forward.

Tilting the shaft toward the target will decrease, or "close," the loft of the club face. Turn or adjust the face of the club into a square position.

4 Position your eyes over the target line.

Lean your body forward from the hips so your eyes are directly above the target line. You should be able to see the alignment of the club's face more easily from this position, increasing your chance of making quality contact and rolling the ball with the proper spin.

5 Do not hit the sweet spot.

Hitting the ball thin, or low on the face, will give you better control over the distance that you are trying to cover.

6 Hit smoothly.

Make an even-paced, smoothly accelerating, and rhythmic stroke, not a popping jerk or a jab. Focus on getting the distance right on longer putts rather than on getting the line exactly right.

HOW TO DRIVE
WITH A PUTTER

1 Use a sturdy, flange-type putter.
Most modern putters are not built to handle the force
that driving a golf ball produces. Try to use a heavier
putter, preferably one with a steel shaft inserted
securely into (rather than over) a thick hosel.

2 Tee the ball up high.
Since a putter does not have any loft, you will have to
tee the ball up high, approximately $1\frac{1}{2}$ to 2 inches off
the ground.

3 Play the ball well forward in your stance.
Tee the ball forward of your front shoulder.

4 Take several practice swings to get the feel of
swinging a putter.
Putters are very light and will fly around much faster
than a driver, and with much less effort.

5 Make solid contact with the ball.
Hit the ball on the upswing. Hitting cleanly is much
more important than swinging hard when driving
with a putter.

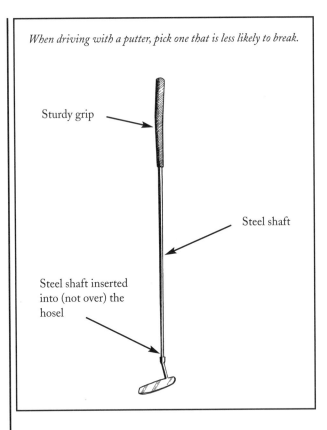

When driving with a putter, pick one that is less likely to break.

Sturdy grip

Steel shaft

Steel shaft inserted
into (not over) the
hosel

Be Aware

- Older, major-brand putters are less likely to break apart on impact. Used-club shops and club repair shops are the best places for finding a putter of this type, but you may find one in a sporting goods store.
- There is a danger that upon contact with the ball, the head of the putter will fly off the shaft. Make sure no one in your group is down course.

HOW TO KEEP SCORE WITHOUT A PENCIL

⭐ Use mental tabulation to keep track of the number of shots over or under par you are for the round. Start at zero. If after the first hole you are two shots over par, you should remember your score as +2. After the second hole, if you are one shot under par, your score is +2-1, or 1. Shooting par does not change your total (+/- 0). At the end of the round, take the course's total par and add or subtract the final number (72 + 9, for example). This method will only assess your cumulative score for the round. It will not help you keep track of your score on each hole.

⭐ Use an alternate writing implement.
- GOLF TEE—Scratch your score onto the scorecard using the pointed end of a golf tee. Press hard to make the number visible. Rubbing dirt lightly over the scorecard and blowing away the excess may make the numbers more legible.
- STICK OR KEY—Use the pointed end of a piece of wood or a key to scratch out your score. If you are unable to read the scratch marks, dip the key or small pointed stick into mud or wet dirt, then mark your score onto the card. If you have a match and can char the end of the stick, this may also help. You may also be able to use the charred end of the match itself.

Mark the card by running your fingernail over a blade of grass.

Use the end of a stick dipped in mud.

- **GRASS OR FRESH LEAF**—Find a wide blade of grass or a leaf, position it over the scorecard, and run a fingernail over it to leave a stain of a number or hash marks representing your score.
- **MAKEUP**—Lipstick, eyebrow pencil, or mascara may also work as a writing implement.

HOW TO GET A CLUB OUT OF A TREE

1 Attempt to shake the tree.
Depending on the size of the tree and the thickness of its trunk, you may be able to dislodge the club by gently shaking the tree. Take care to avoid being hit by the club when it falls.

2 Try to dislodge the club using a ball retriever, flag-stick, or another club.
Someone in your group may have a telescoping ball retriever, or, if you are near the green, grab the flag-stick. Use the implement to reach the club or shake the branch where it is lodged.

3 Create a longer poker.
Secure the flagstick to a golf club or to a telescoping ball retriever using athletic tape, shoelaces, or band-ages. Tie the grip of the club to the base of the flagstick. Hold the head of the club and use the flag end of the stick to knock the club loose.

4 Climb the tree.
Use this method only if you cannot dislodge the club with the above methods, the tree is easily climbable, and the club is not too high. Carry another club in your belt to help you reach the stuck club or the branch that it is resting on, or have another player

Try to dislodge the club using a ball retriever, flagstick, another club, or a combination of these items.

chapter 2: equipment disasters

hand up a club when you are in position. See "How to Retrieve a Ball Stuck in a Tree" (page 24) for correct tree-climbing technique.

Be Aware

- Tossing other clubs into the tree in an attempt to dislodge the lost club may result in multiple stuck clubs or damage to the clubs.
- Do not throw sticks and stones at the errant club. They are not very effective and may hit you or members of your party on the way down.

HOW TO SURVIVE IF YOU RUN OUT OF TEES

★ Look for discarded or broken tees.
Golf courses are often littered with broken tees. You may be able to find one with a long enough head, or one that you can easily repair with a bit of tape or gum.

★ Build a pyramid of wet sand or dirt.
Before the advent of plastic and wooden tees, golfers used sand to get the ball off the ground. If no sand is available, try using moist dirt from the rough to build your pyramid. Make certain the dirt does not contain pebbles or rocks that may alter your shot or fly down the course with your ball. Drive normally.

★ Use smashed ground.
Before your shot, swing the club face, leading edge down, into the ground. This will cause the turf to wedge up, creating a small mound on which you can place your ball.

★ Use small sticks.
Collect several sticks and build a pyramid. Gently place the ball on the pile.

The Rule

A player is not required to use a tee on the first shot, but has the option of doing so.

Repair a broken tee using gum or tape.

Build a pyramid out of sticks or dirt.

DANGEROUS
ANIMALS

HOW TO DEAL WITH AN ALLIGATOR NEAR YOUR BALL

1 Determine the size of the alligator.

Although even small alligators can cause injury, those less than four feet long are not as dangerous to humans. If the alligator is larger than six feet, be especially wary, as a bite can inflict major damage. Alligators larger than nine feet should be considered deadly.

2 Calculate the distance from the alligator to your ball.

The immediate danger zone is within 15 feet of an alligator.

3 Try to determine if the alligator sees your ball.

Alligators are attracted to objects that appear to be food. Golf balls look like alligator eggs, which alligators eat.

4 Do not stand between the alligator and water.

If disturbed, an alligator on land will seek refuge in water. Make sure the alligator is between you and any nearby water hazard.

5 Make a loud noise.

Alligators are sensitive to loud noises. Yelling or screaming may cause the animal to leave. If the alligator does not move, however, you will have gained its attention.

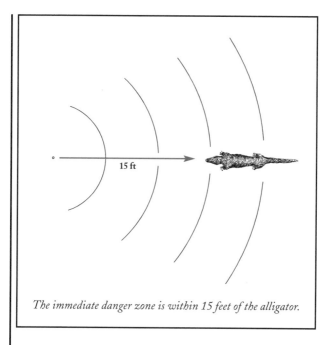

The immediate danger zone is within 15 feet of the alligator.

6 Use a ball retriever to recover the ball.
The alligator may lunge and bite at objects that invade its space. A telescoping ball retriever, best used when the alligator is not facing you or the ball, can quietly scoop up the ball. You can also use a flagstick, though you will have to use it to roll the ball out of the way.

7 Quickly move away from the alligator's territory.
After retrieving the ball, or if you encounter difficulties, run. While alligators can move fast, they generally will travel only short distances and probably cannot outrun an adult golfer.

Be Aware

- Alligators are common on golf courses throughout the Gulf Coast states in the United States, and can be found as far north as North Carolina. To be safe, assume that any body of water on a course in these states is home to an alligator.
- Never wade into a water hazard on a golf course known to be home to alligators. You are most likely to be attacked in or at the edge of water.
- Be especially wary during spring months, when alligators wander in search of mates, and during late summer, when eggs hatch. Mother alligators will respond aggressively to threats to their young, and any adult alligator may come to the aid of any youngster.
- An alligator more than nine feet long is likely to be male, and males tend to move around more and be more aggressive.
- Do not assume any alligator is safe to approach. While some animals may be habituated to the presence of humans, alligators are wild animals, and therefore unpredictable: they may attack without provocation.

HOW TO DEAL
WITH A SNAKE
NEAR YOUR BALL

1 Observe the color pattern and markings of the snake—from at least six feet away.

All snakes should be considered dangerous. Although there is no universal way to determine whether a snake is venomous from its markings, there are some species that can be identified and should be avoided.

In the United States, watch for:
• Rattlesnakes, which are instantly recognizable by the rattle on the tail.
• Copperheads, which have a distinctive pattern of hourglass-shaped bands down the back.
• Water moccasins, which lack any single feature that allows them to be immediately identified except that they will open their mouths wide when disturbed, exposing the white interior (hence their nickname, "cotton mouth").
• Coral snakes, which have repeating colored bands of black, yellow, and red—in that order.

Outside the United States, you may encounter:
• Cobras (Asia, Africa, and India), which flare a hood below their heads when disturbed. The hood may not be noticeable if the snake is calm. A cobra will rear up and "stand" when threatened, and

some types may spit venom up to several feet, aiming for the eyes. The venom can cause blindness.

- Kraits (Southeast Asia and India), which may be "common" (black with white bands) or "banded" (alternate black and yellow bands). Both have hexagonal scales along the ridge of the back, though these may be difficult to see from a distance.
- Tiger snakes (Australia, Tasmania, and surrounding islands), which vary in color, will raise their heads, flatten their necks, and hiss loudly when threatened.

2 If the snake appears to be one of these species, take a drop.
You should sacrifice your ball, but you do not need to sacrifice a stroke penalty: the rules allow a free drop to avoid dangerous animals.

3 If the snake is coiled, this is a sign that it is ready to strike—leave it alone and take a drop.
A coral snake can strike from what appears to be a relaxed posture, however.

4 Stand still.
If the snake does not feel threatened but is intimidated by the sight of you, it may leave the area on its own. Give it time to move away before attempting any ball retrieval measures. Do not try to scare the snake, however, or it is more likely to react defensively.

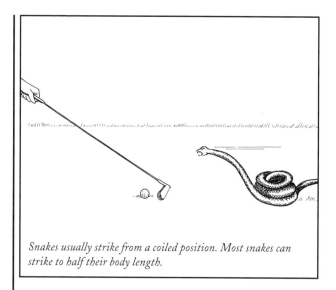

Snakes usually strike from a coiled position. Most snakes can strike to half their body length.

5 If the snake remains, is not coiled, and does not appear to be venomous, estimate its length before attempting to retrieve your ball.

If the snake is five feet long or shorter, use your club or a telescoping ball retriever to get your ball. A snake of this size should not be able to strike beyond the length of a golf club. Most snakes can strike half their body length. If the snake is longer than five feet, use a tree branch at least four feet long to retrieve your ball.

Be Aware

• Snakes can be encountered at any time of day in the spring or fall. During summer when temperatures rise, snakes are more active in the morning or late afternoon.

- Some nonvenomous snakes imitate the coral snake, but have a band pattern in the following color order: black, yellow, black, red.
- A golf glove will not provide sufficient protection to prevent a snake's fangs from entering your skin.
- Most deaths by snakebite are due to allergic reactions and lack of rapid medical treatment after a bite. Although a snakebite should be considered a medical emergency and treatment should be sought immediately, deaths from snakebites are extremely rare. There are thousands of bites each year in the United States but only a few dozen deaths.

HOW TO SPOT A RABID ANIMAL

1 Watch out for raccoons, skunks, and bats.
All warm-blooded animals can carry rabies, but the disease is most common among these animals. Coyotes, foxes, and larger rodents, such as groundhogs, can also carry rabies. It is rare among mice, squirrels, chipmunks, guinea pigs, hamsters, rabbits, rats, and other small rodents.

2 If the animal is foaming or appears to have a locked jaw, stay away.
There are two type of rabies: "furious" rabies and "dumb" rabies. Animals with the former are hostile, may snap and bite, and have an increase in saliva, which makes their mouths appear to be foaming. Animals with the latter (also called paralytic rabies) are timid and shy, and may have paralysis of the lower jaw and muscles.

3 If you are bitten by any animal, immediately wash the bite out with soap and running warm water.
The wound can also be treated with an antiseptic such as hydrogen peroxide or an antibiotic ointment. Dress the wound with a sterile cloth or bandage, and put pressure on the wound to stop bleeding. Get professional medical attention as soon as possible.

4 | Call animal control authorities to report the incident. Describe the animal and where you were when you received the bite so that they can try to catch the animal. Tests will determine if the animal has rabies. Without the animal to test, the medical treatment may mean painful injections, since health providers will have to assume the animal had rabies. Do not try to catch the animal yourself.

5 | Monitor your health.
Early symptoms of rabies include mental depression, restlessness, and abnormal sensations such as itching around the site of the bite, headache, fever, tiredness, nausea, sore throat, or loss of appetite. Other early symptoms include muscle stiffness, dilation of pupils, increased production of saliva, and unusual sensitivity to sound, light, and changes of temperature. Symptoms usually develop within two to eight weeks after infection. The more severe the bite, the sooner the onset of symptoms.

Be Aware

Generally, you will know if a wild animal has bitten you. However, bat bites can be small and may not be felt. A bat that is active by day, that is found in a place where bats are not usually seen, or that is unable to fly is far more likely to be rabid.

HOW TO REMOVE A TICK

Because you will probably not feel a tick biting you, it's a good practice to check yourself for ticks thoroughly after every round of golf.

1 Locate the tick.

Look for a small bump on the skin, similar to the last remnants of a scab before it heals. Ticks vary in size from the head of a pin to a fingernail (when they are engorged) depending on the type and the stage of maturity. Ticks are usually brown or reddish. Check behind the knee, between fingers and toes, in the underarms, in the belly button, in and behind the ear, on the neck, in the hairline, and on the top of the head.

When engorged, ticks can be as large as your fingernail.

Jaws

2 Act quickly to remove the tick.

Use a commercially available tick removal tool if one is available. Follow the instructions that come with the device. If no tick removal device is available, locate a pair of medium- or fine-tipped tweezers.

3 Place the tip of the tweezers around the area where the jaws of the tick enter the skin.

Using a slow, steady motion, pull the tick away from the skin. Do not jerk, crush, squeeze, or puncture the tick, because more pathogens from the tick may get into the wound. If part of the tick breaks off, try to remove it as you would a splinter. Your body will naturally eject the foreign material over time, so leave it alone if you cannot remove it easily.

Place the tweezers around the tick where its jaws enter the skin. Pull with a slow, steady motion.

4 If no tweezers are available, use the nails of your index finger and thumb.

Avoid touching the tick with your skin; use latex gloves, plastic baggies, or even paper towels to cover the skin of your fingers. If nothing to protect your skin is available, try using two credit cards as tweezers: squeeze the edges together to grab the tick and then pull firmly away from the skin. Failing this, it is better to remove the tick with bare forefinger and thumb than to leave it attached.

5 Immediately disinfect the area around the bite with soap and water, alcohol, or antibacterial ointment. If you carry club-cleaning fluid in your bag, this may suffice until other disinfection means are available.

6 Place the tick, dead or alive, in a sealable container. Include a lightly moistened paper towel. Take the tick to a local health department to be analyzed, to determine if it is carrying disease.

HOW TO RECOGNIZE LYME DISEASE

Watch for these symptoms:
- A round, "bull's eye" rash on the skin, which may be very small or up to twelve inches across.
- Other rashes or skin bruising that can mimic common skin problems, including hives, eczema, sunburn, poison ivy, and flea bites. The rash may itch or feel hot, and it may disappear and return several weeks later. The rash will look like a bruise on people with dark skin color.

- Flu-like symptoms several days or weeks after a bite from an infected tick: aches and pains in the muscles and joints, low-grade fever, and fatigue.
- Other systemic symptoms, which can affect virtually any organ in the body, including jaw pain and difficulty chewing; frequent or painful urination and/or repeated urinary tract infections; respiratory infection, cough, asthma, and pneumonia; ear pain, hearing loss, ringing, sensitivity to noise; sore throat, swollen glands, cough, hoarseness, difficulty swallowing; headaches, facial paralysis, seizures, meningitis, stiff neck; burning, tingling, or prickling sensations; loss of reflexes, loss of coordination; stomach pain, diarrhea, nausea, vomiting, abdominal cramps, loss of appetite; and irregular heartbeat, palpitations, fainting, shortness of breath, and chest pain.

Be Aware

- Tucking your pants into your socks is a good preventive measure against ticks.
- Ticks do not drop from high vegetation or trees; they climb up your body, generally seeking the highest point on the body. However, if the tick meets resistance, it will stop and feed at that point.
- Ticks are most active in the spring and early summer, though they may be present at other times of the year.
- Ticks are found in virtually all climates and geographic regions, from the Antarctic to the Sahara. They will often be most abundant in areas with wildlife, whose blood provides their food supply.

- On the golf course, stay on the fairway and out of the rough to avoid ticks.
- Ticks can be difficult to remove, and improper removal can cause tick mouthparts to remain in the skin and/or pathogens from the tick's body to enter the bloodstream. In particular, small, immature ticks (called larvae or nymphs) can be very hard to remove in one piece.
- Lyme disease is treatable with antibiotics—and the sooner treatment begins, the better.

HOW TO SURVIVE A BIRD ATTACK

1 Watch for hovering and clacking.
To intimidate predators, many species will hover and clack their beaks before attacking. If you observe this behavior, be ready for a bird attack.

2 Close your eyes and cover your ears.
A bird will swoop down quickly, striking at the head or shoulders with its wings or beak.

3 Run for cover away from nesting and foraging areas.
Run as fast as you can onto the green or fairway and away from the area, most likely in the rough, that the bird is protecting. Many species will attack if their nests or foraging areas are disturbed, even incidentally. If a bird attacks, it will continue to attack until you leave these areas. Continue to cover your ears while running.

Be Aware
- Wearing a hat can offer some protection to your head against attacks.
- Ducks and geese are notorious for going after people. They can approach noisily, heads high. When attacking, they will lower their heads, hiss and charge, and can tear exposed flesh with their sharp beaks.

Cover your eyes and ears and run as fast as you can.

- Many species of bird common to golf courses will attack a human, particularly mockingbirds, blackbirds, and magpies.
- Do not carry food. Birds habituated to human contact, including seagulls and crows, will swoop down and bite at foods and the fingers that hold them, particularly if the person is gesticulating with the food.
- Birds and other wildlife found on golf courses are generally protected by law. Never use a golf club as a weapon against them.
- Do not assume it is safe to approach a nest just because no adult bird is in sight; eggs demand careful temperature regulation and adults are generally close by. Wild birds nest—and eggs hatch—during the spring, so be particularly careful when golfing at this time.
- While golfing in Australia, beware the cassowary. These flightless, ostrich-size birds may attack small humans when hungry.

HOW TO SURVIVE IF YOU HIT A BEEHIVE

1 Get ready to act as soon as you realize that you have hit a hive.

Striking a hive or nest with a ball or club will likely provoke a strong defensive response from the bees.

2 Do not swat.

Never swat at honeybees or wasps. Swatting may incite them to sting when they otherwise had no intention of doing so.

3 Run from the nest.

Bees and wasps can fly faster than you can run. However, the farther you get from the nest, the less likely they will be to follow you. When you are stung by a bee or wasp, you are marked with an alarm pheromone and other bees and wasps will continue the attack in response to the chemical. The intensity of the attack will continue to increase if you do not continue fleeing the hive area. Extremely defensive colonies may pursue you for half a mile.

4 Cover your face and head with your shirt or jacket.

Bees and wasps usually focus their attack on the head and face. While running, pull your shirt or jacket up over your head, leaving only a small slit to see where you are going. A honeybee will lose its stinger and die once it stings, but a wasp can sting multiple times.

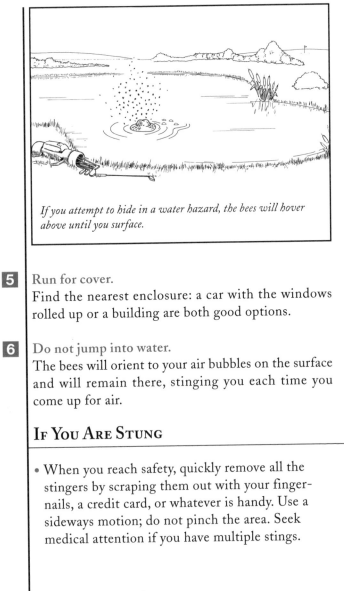

If you attempt to hide in a water hazard, the bees will hover above until you surface.

5 | Run for cover.
Find the nearest enclosure: a car with the windows rolled up or a building are both good options.

6 | Do not jump into water.
The bees will orient to your air bubbles on the surface and will remain there, stinging you each time you come up for air.

IF YOU ARE STUNG

- When you reach safety, quickly remove all the stingers by scraping them out with your finger-nails, a credit card, or whatever is handy. Use a sideways motion; do not pinch the area. Seek medical attention if you have multiple stings.

- Do not wear body fragrances such as scented creams, perfumes, and after-shave lotions. They may attract bees, and may incite an attack.
- Do not blow at or near a hive; bee and some wasp colonies react defensively to mammalian breath.
- Look for head-butting. Extremely defensive honey bee colonies will have a few bees patrolling the immediate vicinity of the nest. When approached they will begin to head-butt you in an effort to encourage you to leave. If this occurs, leave the area immediately.

Be Aware

- Honeybee colonies are commonly located in dark cavities in buildings, water valve boxes, and utility equipment, as well as in ground holes and cavities in trees. Usually the small entrance hole is all that is visible.
- Honeybee colonies are perennial, while wasp colonies develop in the spring and die in the fall. Both wasp and bee colonies reach their population zenith during the summer months.
- Vibrations from a golf cart may elicit a defensive reaction from the hive or nest.
- A swarm of honeybees may settle on a tree branch or on the overhang of a structure. These bees are looking for a new home, and such swarms are not usually defensive.

- Wasp colonies are usually much smaller than those of bees, and their paper nests are often exposed, leaving them more easily disturbed. Some wasp species build large enclosed nests that hang from tree branches.

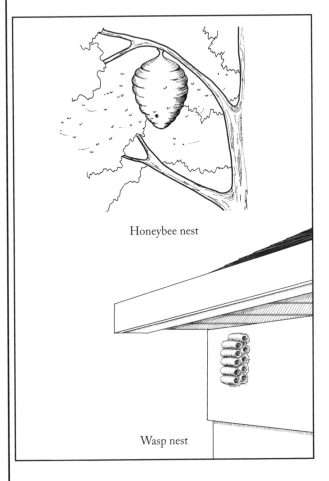

Honeybee nest

Wasp nest

chapter 3: dangerous animals

HOW TO DISARM
AN IRATE GOLFER

1 Determine the level of danger.
If a golfer is waving a club around angrily or drunkenly, or is exhibiting undue hostility, it may be necessary to act quickly to restore order and safety.

2 Try to talk him down.
Speak calmly, keeping your tone even and your voice low. Do not make sudden gestures or movements. Remind him that it's only a game. Tell him to take a few deep breaths.

3 If he threathens to strike, quickly move into the center of the potential swing.
As he draws the club back to swing at you, approach him at an angle that will bring you to the center of the club. Try to remain close to his body. You are much more likely to be injured by the outer end of the club.

4 Grab the club.
At the top of his swing, or just as the club starts to descend, step close to him and, using one or both hands, clutch the club tightly near the grip. Pull down, staying close to him, until you can wrap your arm around the club. Hold the shaft with your armpit while keeping a firm grasp on the club's grip.

Grab here.

Grab the club of the irate golfer as it starts to descend or at the top of the swing.

Tuck the club under your armpit and wrench it away by rotating away from the irate golfer.

5 | Wrench the club away.
Maintaining your hold, rotate your body around, away from the golfer's face. This maneuver should give you the leverage you need to wrench the club out of his grip. Pull with just enough force to free the club from his grasp.

6 | Step back quickly, and be prepared for him to continue to be angry and to flail.
If necessary, use the club to keep him away from his bag, where he might obtain a second weapon.

7 | If necessary, call for help.
Seek the assistance of your fellow golfers to help defuse the situation.

8 | Continue to talk to him until he calms down.

Be Aware

It is always advisable to make all possible attempts to avoid physical confrontation. Your first choice should be to ignore and walk away from an irate golfer. Your next choice should be to use verbal skills to calm the golfer by speaking in low tones and showing understanding. Become physical only as a last resort, to avoid greater injury to yourself or others.

HOW TO CONTROL YOUR GOLF RAGE

1 Immediately set down anything you might be inclined to break or use as a weapon.
Drop your clubs, bags, balls, spike-cleaning tools, golf shoes—anything you might use to injure another golfer.

2 Take ten deep breaths.
Breathe by expanding your stomach and abdomen, not your chest. This will cause the oxygen to enter your bloodstream more quickly, calming you down.

3 Repeat the following words to yourself as you breathe: "It's just a game. It's just a game."
Putting the cause of your anger in perspective may help prevent you from causing harm.

4 If you feel you have been wronged, say so.
Be polite but assertive—explain clearly to the person involved why you are angry. Limit the discussion to the specific cause of your anger—do not get into bigger issues such as, "You always act this way."

5 Avoid making inflammatory statements.
Making value-judgment and personal insults or implying illegal tactics will not be helpful.

6 Listen and tolerate.

Inevitably, the object of your anger will have a few thoughts of his own. Let him talk—this will decrease the likelihood of a further argument, and increase the likelihood of a resolution. Try to see the situation through the other person's eyes, even if this is difficult. The person you are speaking with will likely follow suit.

7 Forgive yourself or the other person for the infraction.

8 Laugh it off.

Try to defuse the situation with humor. Laughter, especially when it comes to golf, is often the best medicine.

Be Aware

However tempting it may be, taking your anger out on an inanimate object such as your clubs, your ball, or your golf cart may only lead to you hurting yourself or irreparably damaging the object. To release your anger, squeeze a golf ball or a plush toy you carry for this purpose.

Chapter 4

GOLFING
EMERGENCIES

HOW TO PREVENT A CLUB FROM FLYING OUT OF YOUR HANDS

⭐ Dry the grip in the sun.
If the grip is wet, or if there is a lot of moisture in the air, leave the club in the hot sun for as long as possible so the moisture will evaporate. Place the club on a hard surface like rock or concrete, which retains more heat than grass and will expedite the drying process.

⭐ Wear gloves.
Golf gloves provide added grip (and reduce chafing and blisters). If no golf gloves are available, thoroughly wet a pair of thin cotton gloves and wear them.

⭐ Rub dry dirt, chalk (magnesium carbonate), talcum powder, cornstarch, dry crumbs, or a powdery stick antiperspirant on sweaty hands or the grip.
These items will absorb excess moisture.

⭐ Rub a slippery grip on sandpaper or concrete to scuff the grip.

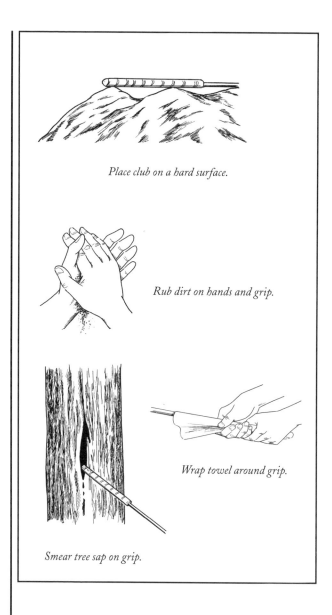

Place club on a hard surface.

Rub dirt on hands and grip.

Wrap towel around grip.

Smear tree sap on grip.

how to prevent a club from flying out of your hands

★ Smear tree sap on the grip to make it sticky.
Sugar maples are good sources of sap in the spring and early summer, when it may run down the sides of the tree. You will be able to find sap from pines or other conifers (spruce, fir) any time of year, and can use it either dried or weeping. Sap can also be found on needles and cones. Note that sap is extremely sticky, and removing it from the skin and other objects will require the use of mineral spirits.

★ Use a towel.
Wrap a handkerchief or a thin towel around the grip of your club when hitting. This is perfectly legal, according to the rules.

HOW TO AVOID GETTING HIT BY A BALL

1 Listen for the shout "Fore!"
Whether the call comes in your direction or not, do not hesitate to react.

2 Do not look for the ball.
Looking up may expose your face and head. Do not attempt to dodge an incoming ball.

3 Turn away from the source of the call.

4 Drop your clubs or stop your cart.

5 Cover your head with your hands and arms.
Put your hands on the back of your head. Bend your arms around the top and sides of your head and tuck it into your chest.

6 Crouch, squat, or drop to the ground.
Roll yourself into a tight ball. If you cannot get to the ground, fold your upper body into itself and bend over.

Drop your clubs, cover your head, and roll into a ball on the ground as soon as you hear "Fore!"

Be Aware

If you and your group are standing on or near the green and the group behind you is hitting up, do one of the following:

- Shield your eyes from the sun so you can easily watch their shots.
- Cover your head and crouch if you lose sight of the ball.
- Get behind your cart, golf bag, caddie, or another nearby object.

HOW TO SURVIVE BEING HIT IN THE GOOLIES

"Goolies" is a Scottish term, used at St. Andrews and elsewhere, that refers to the "privates," or the groin area.

1 Lie down immediately.
Do not walk around. Cover your private parts to shield the area from further injury (and embarrassment). Clutching yourself will probably be your natural reaction to being hit by a club head or ball.

2 Apply a cold pack to the injured area to reduce swelling.
Use ice in a bag or cloth, or a cold can of soda or beer. This will help reduce the swelling and the pain.

3 Do not apply too much pressure.
Extreme pressure may cause more pain.

4 If the pain is significant and does not subside within a few minutes, inspect the injury.
Remove your pants to get a better look at the swelling and check for any irregularities.

5 If the pain lasts more than an hour, or if the area is significantly bruised, seek medical attention.

HOW TO CARRY AN INJURED GOLFER

IF ALONE

Use the "fireman's carry" to bring the golfer to safety.

1 Face the injured person.

2 Prop the victim upright in a sitting or partly standing position.
Bend down so your shoulder is level with her waist.

3 Lean into her body.
Have the injured golfer bend forward over your shoulder so her head and arms are behind you and her legs are in front of you.

4 Put your arms around her legs and stand up.
The victim should be bent at the waist over your shoulder, head behind, with legs in front of you.

5 Walk the victim to the clubhouse.
You should be able to walk a fair distance like this, as weight distribution is over your back and legs instead of your arms.

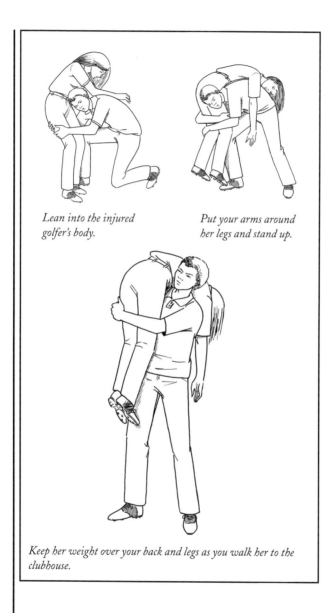

Lean into the injured
golfer's body.

Put your arms around
her legs and stand up.

Keep her weight over your back and legs as you walk her to the
clubhouse.

If Accompanied by Another Person

Use the "deadlift carry" when you have the aid of another person.

1 Lay the injured golfer on his back.
Alternatively, the injured golfer could be sitting upright on the ground.

2 Stand behind the injured golfer.
Your carrying partner should be facing you on the other side of the victim, near his legs.

3 Kneel down.

4 Slide your arms under the victim's arms and wrap them around his chest.

5 Instruct your partner to kneel between the victim's legs.
Your partner should place her arms under the victim's knees, as if she were lifting the handles of a wheelbarrow to push it.

6 Stand up.
You and your carrying partner should rise at the same time. You will have about two-thirds of the victim's weight and your partner will have the rest.

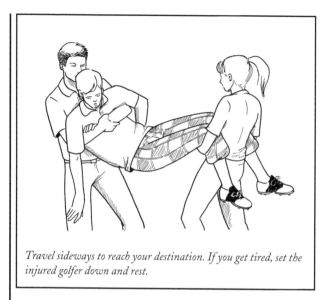

Travel sideways to reach your destination. If you get tired, set the injured golfer down and rest.

7 | Walk to get help.
This position is difficult to maintain for long distances. If you get tired, it is easier to sit the injured golfer down and pick him up again using this method than with the one-person fireman's carry.

HOW TO TREAT A SPRAINED ANKLE

1 Sit or lie down immediately.
Do not put any weight on the ankle.

2 Make a cold compress.
Cold will constrict blood vessels and reduce swelling.
Place ice in a plastic bag or wrap it in a shirt. Do not
apply the compress directly to the skin; add a layer
of clothing or plastic to prevent freezing of tissue.
Applying cold cans may also reduce swelling.

3 Elevate the ankle.
Sit down and raise the ankle at least 18 inches above
the ground by putting a log, golf bag, or other object
under the calf.

Apply cold to reduce swelling.

4 | Apply the compress for 30 minutes, then remove.
If the sprain is particularly bad and swelling is rapid and severe, leave the compress on for 15 additional minutes.

5 | Make a pressure bandage.
If no emergency bandage is available, cut or tear cloth into long, four-inch-wide strips. Two three-foot strips should be sufficient. If available, use an elastic wrap.

6 | Wrap the ankle.
Put one end of the bandage in the middle of the foot and use a figure-eight pattern to wrap up and over the ankle and back around the foot. Make sure the bandage is snug and the ankle immobile. Use tape, rubber bands, string, or shoelaces to secure the end of the bandage to the leg.

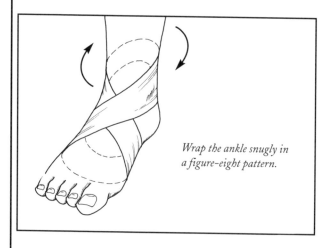

Wrap the ankle snugly in a figure-eight pattern.

| *how to treat a sprained ankle*

7 Reapply the cold compress for another 30 minutes.

8 Leave the course.
Use a golf cart to reach the clubhouse. If no cart is available, use an umbrella, ball retriever, sturdy tree branch, or sand wedge as a cane for support.

9 Take ibuprofen to reduce the swelling and relieve pain.
If ibuprofen is not available, take acetaminophen, which will relieve pain but not swelling. Avoid aspirin, which can thin the blood.

10 Seek medical attention immediately to ensure that the ankle hasn't been broken or fractured.

Be Aware
Sprains are generally a result of tissue damage to the front outside ligaments of the ankle. X-rays are usually not needed for sprained ankles but should be obtained if you are unable to bear weight for more than six steps; if you feel pain in the back of either of the bones that normally protrude from the sides of the ankle; or if you have pain anywhere along the line from your ankle to your smallest toe.

HOW TO TREAT A BLISTER

1 Cover the blister with a bandage.
If you do not have a bandage with you, you can fashion one with a tissue and a piece of adhesive tape or grip tape: fold the tissue until it is just big enough to cover the blister, then tape it. Small blisters (less than three-quarters of an inch) do not usually need any further care.

2 If the blister is large and swollen, prepare to pop it.
Use alcohol (brandy or whiskey from a flask will do the trick) or the flame from a match or lighter to sterilize a needle. Hold the needle in the flame for at least ten seconds.

3 Pierce the blister with the needle.
Hold the needle parallel to the surface of the skin. Puncture the blister near the edge to make draining easier.

4 Drain the fluid.
Gently apply pressure to squeeze out the fluid. Dispose of the needle in a sturdy plastic or metal box so that it does not accidentally prick anyone else.

5 Cover the sore immediately with a bandage.
See step 1. If you have antibiotic cream, use it.

6 Watch for signs of infection.
These include redness, swelling, pain, discharge, and fever. If you have these symptoms, get to a health-care professional.

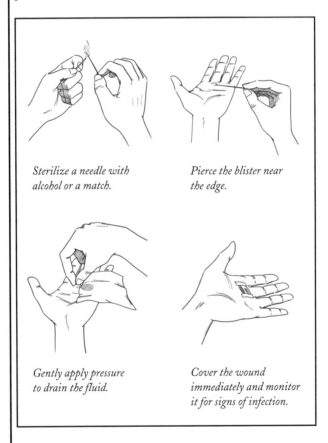

Sterilize a needle with alcohol or a match.

Pierce the blister near the edge.

Gently apply pressure to drain the fluid.

Cover the wound immediately and monitor it for signs of infection.

HOW TO TREAT POISON IVY, POISON OAK, AND POISON SUMAC

1 Wash the exposed area of skin.
Immediately wash the contaminated area with large amounts of running water.

2 Wash shoes, socks, pants, gloves, and clubs immediately.
Urushiol oil, which causes the rash, can stay active on objects for up to a year. Dilute the oil by washing equipment with lots of water. Slosh rubbing alcohol over exposed skin (except on the face) and rinse with water. (Carry a jar containing rubbing alcohol and a small cloth.) Rubbing alcohol neutralizes the oil.

3 Do not scratch the rash.
A rash usually develops a few hours to a few days after exposure. It will start with an itch accompanied by a light rash that continually becomes more intense and eventually blisters. Excessive and continual scratching can lead to neural dermatitis (persistent itch) that can continue even after the reaction has stopped. The total reaction usually lasts two weeks or less. If the itch is intolerable, seek medical assistance.

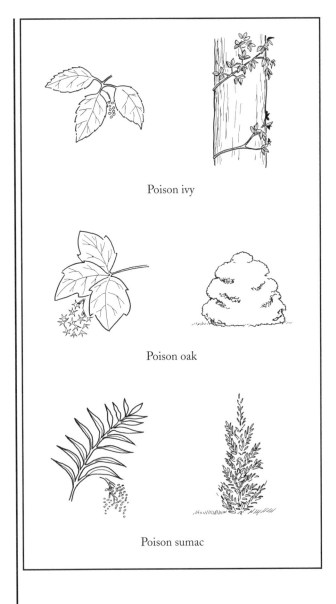

Poison ivy

Poison oak

Poison sumac

chapter 4: golfing emergencies

4 To reduce itching, run hot water over the rash or blister area.

Gradually increase the temperature of the water (be careful not to burn yourself). Let the water run hot until you feel bursts of relief from the area, which may take five minutes or more. Hot water helps to release histamines from the skin. This method can relieve itching for eight hours or more. Warm or cold packs and calamine lotion can also reduce itching. Prescription cortisone cream is many times the strength of over-the-counter cortisone cream and can be used for severe itching.

Be Aware

- Poison ivy and oak thrive in disturbed ground, such as land molded and shaped for golf courses; be sure to ask if it is present on the course before beginning your round. Size and appearance of poison ivy and oak varies with habitat. Poison sumac is fairly rare and limited to deep swamps. Its leaflets can be from two to eight inches long, and the plants can be six inches high, or can vine to the top of a 20-foot-tall tree. All three plants contain urushiol.
- Poison ivy and poison oak grow in all areas of the United States except for southwestern deserts and mountain elevations above 4,000 feet.
- Even when leaves are not present, the stems, berries, and roots of the plants still contain the oil and should be avoided.
- To prevent exposure, wear shoes and socks and long pants, not shorts.

- Do not rub other plants or leaves on an affected area to treat or prevent a rash. There are no plant juices known to neutralize urushiol, and juices spread on the body in small quantities are likely to spread the oil and increase the rash.
- Even if you have not previously reacted to poison ivy, oak, or sumac, do not assume you are immune. After the first exposure, and especially after repeated exposures, 85 percent of people will have an allergic reaction.
- A golf ball that rolls through any of these poisonous plants, or that has come to rest among the leaves or vines of the plants, may be contaminated with urushiol oil. Carefully pick up your ball with a towel or while wearing your glove and wash the ball immediately. Wash the towel or glove before using it again.

HOW TO TREAT SUNBURN

1 Get out of the sun immediately.

2 Do not apply suntan lotion, oil, petroleum jelly, ointment, or butter to the burn.
These will make the symptoms worse and prevent the skin from cooling in the air.

3 Apply a cool compress.
Take off your shirt and soak it in cold water. Dunk it in a water hazard if no other source of water is available. Wear the shirt or hold it on the burned area. (Continue to apply the cool compress once you are at home, or take a cool bath.)

4 Drink water.
Drinking 32 to 64 ounces of water will prevent dehydration and promote sweating.

5 Use a soothing gel or lotion on the skin to cool the burned area.
Aloe works best. If aloe plants grow nearby, break off a leaf and squeeze the gel out directly.

6 Seek medical attention immediately if you experience serious symptoms.
Side effects to watch for include faintness; dizziness; a fast pulse or fast breathing; pale, clammy, or cold skin; sensitivity to light; rash; fever; nausea; or chills.

Be Aware

- Avoid sun exposure between 10:00 A.M. and 2:00 P.M. standard time because the sun is at its hottest during these hours. Remember that the sun's rays are stronger at high altitude and close to the equator.
- Use a sunscreen with an SPF (sun protection factor) of at least 15, and apply it at least 30 minutes prior to exposure.
- If the burn is mild, a hot shower immediately after the burn can cause peeling and actually relieve itchiness more quickly.
- Prolonged exposure to sun and heat can also cause heat exhaustion and/or heatstroke. Heat exhaustion is usually a mild illness brought on by exposure to heat, but heatstroke, which develops beyond the point of heat exhaustion, can be fatal. Symptoms of both include fever and sweating, but an important difference is the presence of mental confusion. If the victim is confused, the illness is no longer heat exhaustion—it is heatstroke.

HOW TO TREAT HEATSTROKE

1 Immediately immerse the victim in cold water.
The core body parts (chest and abdomen) are the most important to cool. Body temperature must be reduced immediately. Heatstroke is usually fatal if not treated rapidly.

2 Remove the victim's clothing and spray the skin with cool misted water while fanning the skin.

Use this method, known as evaporative cooling, only if immersion is impossible. Do not use cold wraps with wet towels, alcohol, or ice cubes; these are not effective cooling measures.

3 Stop the cooling when the body temperature falls below 102° F.

Hypothermia may result if the victim becomes too chilled. In most cases, you will not have access to a thermometer, so continue cooling measures until safe temperatures are confirmed by a health-care professional.

4 Do not administer acetaminophen or aspirin.

Both of these drugs may worsen heatstroke: acetaminophen by damaging the liver, and aspirin by increasing core temperature.

5 Get the victim to a health professional as soon as possible.

How to Prevent Heatstroke

- Wear a light-colored cotton shirt.
- Wet your shirt in cool water to enhance cooling through evaporation.
- Spray misted water on your face, arms, and legs to promote cooling.
- Drink plenty of cold fluids.
- Take frequent shade breaks.

HOW TO AVOID DEHYDRATION

1 Get out of the sun.
Dehydration (actually, volume or fluid depletion) can be caused by excessive perspiration from strenuous activity in hot conditions. Rest frequently in a cool area out of the heat of the sun.

2 Drink water and eat salty foods.
Alternate drinking plain water and consuming salty crackers, pretzels, or water that contains sodium, potassium, and bicarbonate. Water alone will not replace lost electrolytes and should not be taken in excess if thirst is due to exertion or sweating.

3 Make an oral rehydration drink.
If salty snacks are not available to take with plain water, you can make an oral rehydration drink that is superior to any of the available sports drinks. In a quart of water, add one quarter-teaspoon of table salt, one quarter-teaspoon of baking soda, and two table-spoons of sugar. If baking soda is not available, use another quarter-teaspoon of salt instead. If available, add half a cup of citrus juice, coconut water, or a mashed ripe banana. (These contain recommended potassium.) Drink this until your thirst is quenched.

4 Eat sweet snacks high in carbohydrates.
Cookies and other sweet bread products will increase energy. Consume sweet drinks such as orange juice if no snacks are available.

5 Avoid alcohol.
Alcohol may worsen symptoms of volume depletion and should be avoided during excessive sweating.

Be Aware

- Some people will not realize they are fluid depleted until they are nearly unconscious. Drink balanced fluids regularly in hot weather and pay attention to thirst, headaches, dizziness, loss of appetite, darker urine, and fatigue, all signs of volume depletion.
- Severe volume depletion, which can include lethargy or loss of consciousness, may require treatment with specialized sodium-potassium-glucose drinks (oral rehydration therapy) or intravenous fluids.

HOW TO AVOID LIGHTNING

1 Abandon your golf clubs.
Metal and graphite clubs conduct electricity and should not be held or carried.

2 Seek shelter immediately.
A sturdy building offers the best protection. Avoid sheds, isolated trees, and convertible cars. These will not protect you from lightning. Also avoid water and hilltops, as these can increase your chances of being struck by lightning.

3 If no building is nearby, get inside a hard-top automobile.
Roll up all windows and do not make contact with any metal inside the car. Do not get in a golf cart; it does not offer lightning protection.

4 If you are stuck out on the course, find a low spot on the ground away from trees, fences, and poles.
If you are in the woods, take shelter under short trees.

5 Make yourself the smallest target possible.
If you feel your skin start to tingle or your hair stand up on end, squat on the balls of your feet, place your hands over your ears, and lower your head between your knees.

Make yourself the smallest target possible. Stay on the balls of your feet to minimize contact with the ground.

6 Do not lie down.

Stay on the balls of your feet to minimize contact with the ground. Do not crouch with your hands on the ground.

Be Aware

- Stay away from rivers and creek beds during a thunderstorm; more people are killed each year from flash floods than from lightning or any other storm-related phenomenon. If you hear a loud, sustained roar, notice hail, or see the sky become greenish, run for shelter immediately. (See "How to Survive a Tornado" on the following page.)
- Do not use any electrical appliances for the duration of the storm. Use a wired telephone only in an emergency.

HOW TO SURVIVE
A TORNADO

1 Find shelter.
The worst place to be during a tornado is out in the open—as on a golf course. If you cannot get inside a sturdy building, find a ditch and lie flat, covering your head with your hands. A sand trap or bunker is a good spot. Do not attempt to outrun or use a golf cart to outrace a tornado.

2 If inside, go to the basement, storm cellar, or the lowest level of the building.
If you are in a building with no basement, go to a first-floor inner hallway or a small inner room without windows, such as a bathroom or closet. Avoid buildings—including clubhouses—that have eaves. High winds can get under the eaves and blow the roof off.

3 Stay low to the floor.
Very few "missiles" (wind-driven debris) penetrate walls below three feet above ground level.

4 Stay away from windows.
High winds and flying debris can shatter glass. Do not open windows.

5 Move to the center of the room.
Corners attract debris during high winds.

Lie completely flat in a sand trap or ditch. Cover your head.

6 Get under a piece of sturdy furniture.
Find a workbench or a heavy table or desk and hold
on to it. If you are in a bathroom, lie down in a bath-
tub.

Be Aware
• Tornadoes are not always easy to spot. They can be
  nearly invisible, marked only by swirling debris at
  the base of the funnel. An approaching cloud of
  debris can mark the location of a tornado even if
  a funnel is not visible. Some tornadoes are com-
  posed of several mini-funnels.

- A dark, often greenish sky, large hail, or a loud roar can indicate that a tornado is imminent.
- Before a tornado hits, the wind may die down and the air may become still.
- Tornadoes generally occur near the trailing edge of a thunderstorm.
- Tornadoes can occur at any time of the year. In the southern United States, peak tornado season is March through May, while peak season in the northern United States is May through August.
- Tornadoes are most likely to occur between 3:00 and 9:00 P.M. but can occur at any hour.

HOW TO PUT OUT A CIGAR BRUSH FIRE

Brush fires can be started in many ways, but on golf courses, cigars pose a significant risk.

1 Stomp out the fire if it is small enough.
Flames that are larger than your shoe will not be safe to stomp out.

2 Immediately throw water or any other nonflammable liquid on the fire.
Use water from a thermos or cooler, a sports drink, or beer (which has a high water content). Do not use hard liquor, which may only increase the fire's strength.

Small fires may be extinguished by stomping or dousing the flames with water.

Smothering a brush fire with sand or a nonflammable jacket may also be effective.

3 Throw dirt or sand on any remaining flames.

4 Cover the fire and embers completely with a non-flammable blanket or jacket.
Suffocate a fire that is just beginning—but be careful not to fan the flames or feed easily flammable material to the fire.

5 Once the fire appears to be out, stomp on the embers to make certain they are no longer burning.

6 If the fire is still burning, use a cell phone to call the fire department directly—not the clubhouse.
If you have been unable to douse the flames and you do not have a cell phone, head immediately to the clubhouse or an emergency phone to call for help.

How to Avoid Starting a Fire

1 Always carry a cup or bottle of water if you are smoking on the course.
You can use this to quickly extinguish any embers or fires before they get out of control.

2 Never puff on a cigar or cigarette while riding in a golf cart.
The ember, carried by the breeze, may blow into leaves or dried grass, or onto flammable clothing.

3 After lighting a cigar or cigarette, make certain that the match is cold, not just out.
Hold it until it is cold, then break it so that you hold the charred portion before throwing it away.

4 When you are finished smoking, grind out your cigar in the dirt or sand, or drown the cigar in water.
Cover the butt with dirt. Never put out your cigar or cigarette by rubbing it against a stump, log, or other flammable object.

HOW TO CURE A GOLF ADDICTION

1 Examine your behavior.

A golf addict is a person whose life is controlled by golf. You may think you have a problem with golf, but still not think that you are an addict. Ask yourself these questions. The total number of questions that you answer "yes" to is not as important as how you honestly feel about yourself as you answer these questions:

- Do you golf regularly? Do you feel empty inside if you cannot golf at your usual time?
- Do you ever golf alone, or watch golf alone?

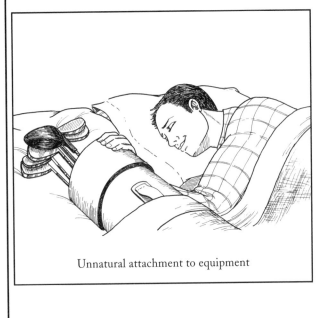

Unnatural attachment to equipment

- Have you ever substituted one club for another, thinking that one particular club was the problem?
- Have you ever cheated to obtain a better score?
- Have you ever lied to get into a golf course of which you were not a member?
- Has your job, family life, or school performance ever suffered from the effects of golf?
- Have you ever been arrested as a result of golf?
- Have you ever lied about the fact that you are playing, or about how much you play?
- Do you put the purchase of golf equipment ahead of your other financial responsibilities?

Watching golf alone

how to cure a golf addiction

- Have you ever suffered a golf-related injury?
- Do you continue to golf despite the fact that you are never satisfied with your performance?
- Does golf interfere with your sleeping or eating?
- Does the thought of not being able to play golf terrify you?
- Do you feel it is impossible for you to live without golf?

2 Admit that you have a problem, and that you need help.

You are not responsible for your disease—but you are responsible for your recovery. You can no longer blame people, places, and courses for your addiction.

Arrested due to golf activities

Playing alone

3 Admit to one other person that you have a problem. This person will help you wean yourself off the game. This person should not be a regular in your foursome.

4 Reduce the amount of golf you play.
Going cold turkey may be difficult—first, reduce by half the number of times you play a week. Then cut that amount in half the following week, and so on. Replace golf with other activities to take your mind off the withdrawal you may experience. Make it a point to play other sports, go to the movies with your family, and watch alternate programming on Sunday afternoons.

5 Make direct amends to everyone you have harmed physically or emotionally as a result of your addiction.

This will help you to "own" your disease, and also allow others to help you when you need it.

6 Watch yourself carefully—and be willing to forgive a relapse.

Many addicts relapse at some point during recovery. If you fall back into your old ways, admit it to yourself first, then to others who can assist you in finding your way again.

7 Do not be afraid to ask for help when you need it.

Your golf pro may be able to direct you to others who have been through what you are dealing with. Form a support group. Therapists may also give you perspective. (Note: Sports therapy is physical therapy, not mental therapy.)

8 Remember that no one is perfect.

Seek the ability to change the things you can, and to accept the things you cannot change. Realize that you may never be able to play golf again without risk of a relapse. There is more to life than golf. But then again, relapses can always be cured.

APPENDIX

RULES AND REGULATIONS

The rules referred to throughout the book are the official rules of the United States Golf Association (USGA). The rules of other national golf associations, including the Royal and Ancient Golf Club of St. Andrews, are consistent with these rules, though the wording may vary.

Subsections of rules are indicated by a dash (Rule 1-4). Official decisions interpret rules, thus Decision 1-4/9 describes the ninth decision regarding the fourth section of Rule 1.

Stroke play rules refer to tournaments that count the total number of strokes per round, which is the more common type of competition. Match play rules apply to competition in which two players go head-to-head; the lowest score on each hole wins that hole. The player who wins the most holes is the winner.

Too Many Clubs

You are allowed to take 14 clubs with you during a round of golf (Rule 4-4). You can take fewer clubs if you wish and add to that number during the round only if the total never exceeds 14. Any added clubs must be yours and not lent to you from anyone on the course. You can share clubs with a partner if the total number of clubs between the two of you is not more than 14 clubs.

If you realize that you have too many clubs in your bag before the start of the round, you can remove the extra clubs. Do not place the extra clubs in your golf cart. The clubs in the golf cart will be added to the number in your bag. If the round has started and you realize you have too many clubs, you must immediately declare the clubs out of play for the remainder of the round. If you do not immediately notify your playing partners that you have more than fourteen clubs, you will be disqualified. The penalty in stroke play for too many clubs is two strokes per hole, with a maximum penalty of four strokes.

BALL HITS BIRD OR BIRD CATCHES BALL

Ball hits bird: Rule 19-1

If you hit a flying bird, it is considered "a rub of the green," also known as tough luck (Rule 19-1). You must play the ball where it lies. If the bird catches the ball in midair and carries it to the green, this is considered fair play, and you can play the ball where it lies.

Ball Lands in or near a Bird's Nest

If your ball lands in or near a bird's nest, you may pick up the ball without penalty. You may not drop your ball any nearer to the hole. You must drop your ball as near as possible to the nest and in a way that would allow you to take your shot without damaging the nest. If the nest is in a hazard, you must drop your ball in the hazard (Decision 1-4/9).

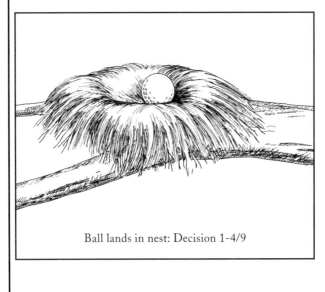

Ball lands in nest: Decision 1-4/9

Using the Wrong Club

There is no such thing as using the wrong club during a round of golf. If you want to tee off with your putter, you can do so without penalty. In general, if the USGA has approved all the clubs in your bag and as long as there are fourteen or fewer clubs, you may use them as you think best.

Using an Illegal Club or Equipment

All clubs in your bag must comply with the standards for golf clubs set by the USGA (Rule 4-1). If a golf club in your bag does not conform to the USGA standards, even if you do not use it, the penalty is disqualification of either the hole or the match.

Specifically, the rules state that you may also not use any artificial device or unusual equipment that might "assist" you in making a stroke or play (including distance gauges and measuring devices), or in gripping a club (other than plain gloves, powder, or a towel or handkerchief).

Fallen Hat Moves Ball

If during stroke play your hat falls off and moves your stationary ball, you are assessed a one-stroke penalty and you must replace the ball to its original location. You are assessed one more stroke if you do not replace it (Rule 18-2).

Hat moves ball:
Rule 18-2

In stroke play, there is no penalty if someone else's hat unintentionally falls and moves your ball. You must replace the ball to its original position. You are assessed a two-stroke penalty if the ball is not replaced.

In match play there is a one-stroke penalty assessed against the player whose hat or whose caddie's hat moves an opponent's ball. It is a loss-of-hole penalty if the opponent does not replace the ball.

OPPONENT MOVES HIS BALL

If your opponent intentionally moves his stationary ball and that movement is not sanctioned by the rules, there is a one-stroke penalty in stroke play and a loss-of-hole penalty in match play (Rule 18-2). There are many situations when a golfer is allowed to move his ball. For example, a player can move the ball to identify it if he announces his intentions and the ball is not in a hazard, or if the ball is located in an area designated as "ground under repair."

BALL LANDS IN MANURE

If your ball lands in manure, you can either play it as it lies or declare it unplayable and take a free drop (Rule 23). If the ball is embedded in the manure, however, there is no free relief. Even though manure is a natural object, the manure is no longer a loose impediment if it is attached to the ball. You will incur a one-stroke penalty if you declare the ball unplayable in this situation.

If your ball lands near or behind a pile of manure, you can move the manure as long as the manure is not embedded in the ground. Rule 23 states that loose

Ball lands in manure: Rule 23

impediments can be removed without penalty. Loose impediments are natural objects such as stones, leaves, twigs, branches, and dung (manure). This also includes worms and insects, and the casts or heaps made by them, provided they are not fixed or growing, are not solidly embedded, and do not adhere to the ball. Sand and loose soil are loose impediments on the putting green but not elsewhere.

USING PUTTER LIKE A POOL CUE

If you hit the golf ball with the top of a club grip as you would hit a pool ball with a pool cue, you will be in violation of Rule 14-1. You would be assessed a two-stroke penalty in stroke play and you would lose the hole in match play. The rule states that you must fairly strike the ball with the head of the club and not

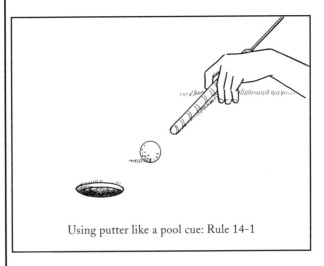

Using putter like a pool cue: Rule 14-1

push, scrape, or spoon the ball. A pool cue shot, even if you used the head of the club, would be considered a push under the rules (Decision 14-1/2).

ANIMAL STEALS YOUR BALL

If a dog, fox, or squirrel steals your ball as it sits on the fairway, you may replace the ball at the original spot without any penalty (Rule 18-1). However, a ball moved by wind or water must be played where it ends up. A snake that moves your ball is considered an outside agency, like a dog or squirrel, but a dead snake is a loose impediment and may be moved if it is blocking your path. Make sure the snake is actually dead. If you are not sure, you can take a free drop.

When a ball has been moved by an animal and it is not clear where its original position was, the player may replace his ball without penalty in an area that provides neither an advantage nor a disadvantage by agreement with opponents (Decision 18-1/5).

Animal steals ball: Rule 18-1

Ball Lands on the Wrong Green

If you hit your ball onto the wrong putting green, you may not hit it off the green. There is no penalty for picking up your ball and dropping it off the green at the nearest point of relief (Rule 25-3). Drop the ball within one club-length of the nearest point of relief but no closer to your intended pin. The nearest point of relief would not include dropping it in a hazard or on the green. You may clean the ball when you lift it from the green.

Ball Leaning against Flagstick

The top of the ball must be below the top of the cup to be considered holed. If the ball comes to rest against the flagstick (but is not holed), the stick may be moved or removed. If the ball falls in, it is considered holed (Rule 17-4). If the ball does not fall in, the player must mark the ball at the edge of the cup. If a player pulls out the stick and the ball is moved away from the hole, that individual must replace the ball without penalty at the edge of the cup. Not replacing the ball is a two-stroke penalty in stroke play and loss-of-hole penalty in match play.

Ball leaning against flagstick: Rule 17-4

FASHION EMERGENCIES

SPLIT SEAM

Use a stapler, safety pin, or tape to repair a split seam.

★ PIN

A safety pin is the fastest, most secure way to hold a seam together. However, many golfers sport lapel pins on their jackets, and these may work in a pinch. Two or three pins in the ripped area should suffice for a temporary solution.

✪ STAPLE

Staples can be used to repair seams and will not damage most fabrics, provided they are removed carefully. Take care to avoid stretching the seam; the fabric may tear around the staples if it is pulled hard. If you are on the course and have any papers with staples already in them, carefully remove the staples and re-use them on the seam. Poke the ends through the fabric and bend them in. Alternatively, the pro shop, restaurant, or clubhouse will most likely have a stapler.

✪ TAPE

Apply very sticky tape to the inside of the garment to hold a seam together. Adhesive tape from a first aid kit should work, though it might mark the garment. Electrical or duct tape will work best. Grip tape for clubs may also be used, but avoid the weaker masking tape and cellophane tape.

BROKEN SHOELACES

✪ SQUARE KNOT

Tie the broken ends of the lace together using a square knot: stack two regular knots, wrapping the same strand over each time. Use the mnemonic "right over left, left over right."

✪ LONGER LACE

Remove the lace and retie it using only the longer end. You may have to skip a few eyelets to have enough length to tie a knot.

⭐ Other laces

If you have carried your street shoes onto the course, they may provide a lace to use in place of the broken one.

⭐ Caddie's laces

If you have a caddie, try borrowing the laces from one of his shoes.

⭐ Golf bag

Use a small strap or tie from your golf bag, if you have one.

Sunglasses That Won't Stay On

⭐ String or a rubber band

Tie a piece of string or a long rubber band between the two ear pieces and stretch it across the back of the head. This will prevent sunglasses from slipping down a sweaty nose.

Alternatively, two rubber bands, one on each side, can be twisted around the earpieces to increase friction and reduce slippage.

⭐ Grip tape

Cut two small pieces of grip tape, which is sticky, and place them on the nose pads on your glasses. The tape will both absorb sweat and keep your glasses from sliding.

A small piece of tissue wedged under the nose pads should prevent slippage, but be aware that it may impair vision.

LOST GLASSES

✪ **BORROW OTHER PEOPLE'S GLASSES**
You may be able to find a pair of glasses from someone who has a similar prescription. You can borrow them when you hit.

✪ **SQUINT**
Squinting actually increases your depth of field by blocking out excess rays entering the retina, allowing images that are fuzzy to become clearer.

✪ **PINHOLE GLASSES**
Pinhole glasses block out excess rays and can improve vision. Draw two circles about the size of a pair of lenses on a piece of paper or cardboard. Use a pin,

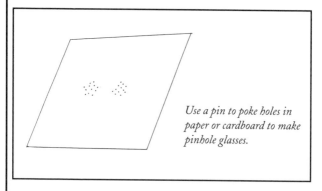

Use a pin to poke holes in paper or cardboard to make pinhole glasses.

Use pinhole glasses to improve your vision.

knife, or a tee to poke at least a dozen small holes in each area where you have drawn your circles. Look through your pinhole glasses to improve your vision.

GAMBLER'S GUIDE

GAME BETS

Bingo Bango Bongo—Each hole is worth three points: one point for hitting the green with the fewest strokes, one point for the player closest to the pin after everyone is on the green (it doesn't matter how many strokes it took to get there), one point for the player in the hole with the fewest number of strokes or to the first player in the hole. A monetary value is assigned to each point, and each player puts that amount in a pot. The player who has the most points at the end of the match wins the pot.

Pick-Up Sticks—Players wager a certain amount for the front nine, the back nine, and the match. Each hole a player loses gives that player the right to remove one of his opponent's clubs from play. The clubs can be brought back into play if that player then loses a future hole (but he cannot then take his opponent's club). Putters can be given "immunity." The winner of each set of holes (and ultimately the match) gets the pot.

Scotch Foursome—Also known as Foursome. Two teams bet a certain amount per hole. Pairs of players alternate shots from tee to green until the ball is in the hole. One player drives even holes and putts odd, the other drives odd holes and putts even. The team who wins the match, the front nine, back nine, or the individual holes (whichever had been decided beforehand) wins the money.

Skins—Each player puts in a certain amount per hole to form a total per-hole pot, or "skin." The player who wins the whole on a net basis (the score for that hole after adjusting for handicap) wins that hole's pot. If any number of players tie, the pot carries over to the next hole, again carrying over until a single player wins a hole. If the 18th hole ends in a tie, the final "skin" goes to the player with the best overall score, a runoff going to the player who won the most "skins." This gambling game is best for threesomes and foursomes.

Snake—The object of this game is to not "three-putt." A player who "three-putts" first "holds the snake." The snake is then held by that player until another player three-putts. At the end of the ninth and eighteenth holes, the player holding the snake must pay the other players a set amount. Combining this game with another gambling game makes life interesting—a player may hit around the green without getting on it to avoid a three-putt, but this may hurt him if another gambling game is being played at the same time.

SIDE BETS

Murphy—A player has declared a "Murphy" when he bets that he can get onto the green and into the hole in a certain number of shots.

Overs—If a player moans about his bad luck, he can be forced to take the shot again if you call an "overs" bet before the ball comes to rest. In this bet, you are betting against that player's ability to do better. If the whiner makes a better shot, he wins. If not, you win.

Scruffy—Calling a "scruffy" is to bet that, despite a horrible tee shot, you can still make par.

Arnie—A bet that is won by scoring par without touching the fairway.

Bambi—A bet that is won by scoring par after hitting an animal.

Froggy—A bet that is won by skipping a golf ball across a water hazard.

GLOSSARY

GOLFSPEAK	TRANSLATION
Looks like I'm stuck on the beach.	I have gotten stuck in a sandtrap/bunker.
You're in the cabbage now.	You are in very thick rough.
That ball's dead.	You are in a position from which you are unable to reach the green.
Well, that's an elephant's ass.	That shot is high, but not very long—and it stinks.
What a goat farm!	This is a very poorly maintained course.
Stop being such a golf lawyer.	Stop constantly telling me the rules.
You left it right in the jaws.	You came just short of the cup.
Now I'm leaking oil.	Now my game is really falling apart.
Don't overcook it.	Do not hit your shot too hard.

You're in throw-up range.	Your putt is close enough to make, but long enough that you will probably miss it.
You burned a few worms on that one.	You have hit a very poor, low shot.
Get up on the dance floor!	Get up onto the putting green!
You're in the soup.	You are in a water trap.
I'm headed for the chopping mall.	I am playing a terrible round.
Nice banana!	That certainly was a big, looping slice!
I fried that egg.	I buried that right in the bunker.
I think I'll use my knife.	I think that I will take that shot with my one iron.
You whiffed that one.	You missed the ball completely.
I think I've got the yips.	I doubt that I can sink short putts.
I guess it's just the rub of the green.	You only have a certain amount of control.

THE EXPERTS

FOREWORD

Jerry Foltz, winner of the 1995 South Carolina Open, is a golf journalist and former touring professional who spent eight years on the Buy.com Tour. He is a weekly columnist for golfonline.com, and has been the on-course commentator for the Golf Channel since 1997.

CHAPTER 1: BAD LIES

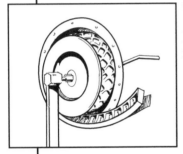

How to Retrieve a Ball Lost in the Washer

Source: Frank Miller is a golf construction and industry consultant. He owns a sod farm and a golf green construction company in Kihei, Hawaii.

How to Tee Off in Front of a Crowd

Sources: Bruce Jackson of Inside/Out in Provo, Utah, is a specialist in performance psychology. His clients include athletes and business leaders • Jim Campbell is the Director of Golf, Cape Cod National Golf Club, Brewster, Massachusetts.

How to Retrieve a Ball Stuck in a Tree

Source: Michael Martinez is a professional tree climber and owner of Specialized Rigging and Tree Care, Inc., a company specializing in the care and maintenance of trees.

How to Retrieve a Ball from a Gopher Hole

Source: Frank Miller.

How to Scale a Fence to Retrieve a Ball
Source: Greg Gaffney is an eleven-year veteran of the Naples, Florida, police force, and an avid fence climber.

How to Play Out of a Water Trap
Source: Jim Campbell.

How to Play Out of High Saw Grass
Source: Mark Heartfield is the head golf professional at the Sankaty Head Golf Club in Siasconset, Massachusetts. In the winter he is director of golf at Orchid Island Golf and Beach Club in Florida.

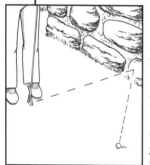

How to Carom the Ball off a Wall
Source: Andrew Campbell is the assistant golf professional at the Merion Golf Club in Ardmore, Pennsylvania.

How to Thwart a Cheat
Source: John Morgan is a professional gambler and a confessed golf cheat who lives in Oakland, California.

How to Stop Thinking about a Horrible Shot
Source: Randall McCracken is a golf pro at Willow Creek Country Club in Salt Lake City, Utah.

How to Stop a Runaway Cart
Source: Mr. X, who prefers to remain anonymous, is a technical representative and trainer for one of the largest golf cart manufacturers in the world. He has worked with electric, gas, turf, and industrial carts for 14 years.

How to Get a Cart Out of a Sand Trap
Sources: Mr. X. • Chad Moore sells and services golf carts at Florida Southern Golf Carts in Brooksville, Florida. • Golf Cars, Inc. in the greater Philadelphia area, Pennsylvania.

How to Start a Dead Cart
Source: Mr. X.

How to Putt with a Driver
Source: Mark Blakemore is a Class A PGA professional with more than 19 years of golf instruction experience. He is the owner and operator of www.PGAProfessional.com, which features free golf tips and articles, handicap calculators, and other golf resources.

How to Drive with a Putter
Source: Mark Blakemore.

How to Keep Score without a Pencil
Source: Paul Attard is a PGA golf professional and is the head of golf at the Brooksville Golf & Country Club in Brooksville, Florida.

How to Get a Club Out of a Tree
Source: Warren Lehr is director of golf at Paa-Ko Ridge Golf Club in Sandia Park, New Mexico.

How to Survive If You Run Out of Tees
Source: Paul Attard.

CHAPTER 3: DANGEROUS ANIMALS

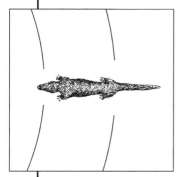

How to Deal with an Alligator Near Your Ball
Source: Kent Vliet, Ph.D., is a faculty member of the Department of Zoology at the University of Florida, Gainesville. He serves as the Coordinator of Labs for the biological sciences program and has studied alligator behavior for twenty years.

How to Deal with a Snake Near Your Ball
Sources: Joseph B. Slowinski was an associate curator of herpetology in the Department of Herpetology at the California Academy of Sciences in San Francisco. He studied venomous snakes in Myanmar (Burma), where he collected cobras, Russell's vipers, kraits, and sea snakes. • Guinevere Wogan is an assistant in the Department of Herpetology at the California Academy of Sciences.

How to Spot a Rabid Animal
Source: Centers for Disease Control.

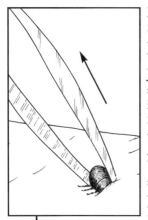

How to Remove a Tick

Sources: Glen Needham, Ph.D., is the codirector of the Ohio State University Acarology Laboratory. • Janet Tobiassen, DVM, is a small-animal veterinarian with a doctorate in veterinary medicine from Oregon State University. She is a member of the American Veterinary Medical Association and serves as the Veterinary Medicine guide at about.com (vetmedicine.about.com). • The Lyme Disease Network of New Jersey, Inc., www.lymenet.org.

How to Survive a Bird Attack

Source: Patty Sprott is an ecologist who disseminates scientific findings of the Long Term Ecological Research Network, a National Science Foundation–funded program. She has studied and written about terrestrial/aquatic interactions among animals, wetland turtles, and bird attacks for the Florida Fish & Wildlife Department. She is online at www.lternet.edu.

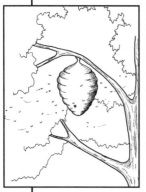

How to Survive If You Hit a Beehive

Source: Eric H. Erickson, Jr., Ph.D., is director of the Carl Hayden Bee Research Center, part of the USDA's Agricultural Research Service. He has 31 years of research experience and is the author of more than 150 scientific publications on honeybee biology and crop pollination.

How to Disarm an Irate Golfer
Source: George Arrington has instructed classes in self-defense for more than 25 years. He holds a fourth-degree black belt and formal teaching license in Danzan-Ryu Jujutsu and has also studied Karate, Aikido, T'ai-chi Ch'uan, Pa Kua, and Hsing-I.

How to Control Your Golf Rage
Sources: Lawrence Arnold, M.D., is a licensed psychotherapist who lives San Bernadino, California. • www.angermgmt.com is a website devoted to anger management. • Victor Bartok is a stress management specialist who lives in New York City.

CHAPTER 4: GOLFING EMERGENCIES

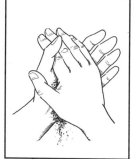

How to Prevent a Club from Flying Out of Your Hands
Sources: Wayne K. Clatterbuck is an associate professor in the department of Forestry, Wildlife & Fisheries at the University of Tennessee's Agricultural Extension Service in Knoxville. • Warren Lehr.

How to Avoid Getting Hit by a Ball
Source: Randall McCracken.

How to Survive Being Hit in the Goolies
Sources: Roger Rosen, M.D., is a general practitioner who lives in Philadelphia, Pennsylvania. • *The American Red Cross First Aid and Safety Handbook* by Kathleen Handal, M.D.

How to Carry an Injured Golfer
Source: James Li, M.D., practitioner in the Division of Emergency Medicine at Harvard Medical School in Cambridge, Massachusetts, is an instructor for the American College of Surgeons' course for physicians, Advanced Trauma Life Support. He is the author of articles on emergency practice in remote settings.

How to Treat a Sprained Ankle
Source: James Li.

How to Treat a Blister
Sources: Roger Rosen. • *The American Red Cross First Aid and Safety Handbook.*

How to Treat Poison Ivy, Poison Oak, and Poison Sumac
Source: Susan Carol Hauser is the author of *Outwitting Poison Ivy: How to Prevent and Treat the Effects of Poison Ivy, Poison Oak, and Poison Sumac*, and *Outwitting Ticks*. She teaches writing at Bemidji State University in Minnesota and is online at www.intraart.com/hauser.

How to Treat Sunburn
Sources: Roger Rosen. • *The American Red Cross First Aid and Safety Handbook.* • *The Complete Idiot's Guide to First Aid Basics.* • James Li.

How to Avoid Dehydration
Source: James Li.

How to Avoid Lightning
Sources: Dave Rust, Ph.D., is a lightning expert at the National Severe Storms Laboratory in Norman, Oklahoma. • John Ogren is the Warning Coordination Meteorologist for the National Weather Service and a specialist in weather safety issues. • *Thunderstorms, Tornadoes, Lightning . . . Nature's Most Severe Storms*, a joint publication of the National Oceanic and Atmospheric Administration, the U.S. Department of Commerce, and the American Red Cross.

How to Survive a Tornado
Sources: Harold Brooks is head of the Mesoscale Applications Group of the National Severe Storms Laboratory in Norman, Oklahoma. He has researched tornadoes and their effects on people for 15 years. • Federal Emergency Management Agency. • National Oceanic and Atmospheric Administration.

How to Put Out a Cigar Brush Fire
Sources: The U.S. National Park Service. • www.fire wise.org is a website devoted to fire-fighting techniques.

How to Cure a Golf Addiction
Source: Adapted from resource material provided by Narcotics Anonymous and Alcoholics Anonymous.

APPENDIX

Rules and Regulations
Sources: USGA Official Golf Rules. • *Rules of Golf* by Tom Watson. • The *Illustrated Golf Rules Dictionary* by Hadyn Rutter.

ACKNOWLEDGMENTS

The authors would like to extend their thanks and the promise of lifelong, good golf karma to all of the experts who contributed their knowledge and experience to this project. Without you we are nothing—or at least we're a lot less knowledgeable.

Joshua Piven thanks all of the experts who contributed their time and golfing expertise, as well as the entire cast of the film *Caddyshack* for their inspiration, wisdom, and creative golf advice.

David "Fuzzy" Borgenicht thanks Jay Schaefer, Steve Mockus, Erin Slonaker, Terry Peterson, Brenda Brown, Joe Borgenicht, and the entire clubhouse at Chronicle Books and Quirk Productions. He would also like to thank his golf-nut grandmother, Helen Sandack, for not getting angry with him at age 10 when he "accidentally" hit her good golf balls into the road behind her house.

Jim Grace thanks his father, Bill Grace, for being an exceptional golfer, and an even better father. He also sends a huge "thank you" to the golf pros who took time out of their full summer days to answer his never-ending list of questions: Andrew Campbell, Jim Campbell, and Mark Heartfield. Finally, he would like to thank his wife, Lisa, and editor, Erin Slonaker, who now know more about golf than they ever wanted to.

ABOUT THE AUTHORS

Joshua Piven is the co-author of three previous *Worst-Case Scenario* books, including *The Worst-Case Scenario Survival Handbook*, which has been translated into more than 20 languages. He continues to work on his golf game, trying to bring his handicap down to double digits. He hopes to one day win all four majors in a single calendar year. He and his wife live in Philadelphia.

David Borgenicht is a writer, editor, and pre-duffer, as well as the co-author of *The Worst-Case Scenario Survival Handbook* series. He lives in Philadelphia with his wife, and has been known to act as her caddie—or he at least carries her bags and follows her around a lot.

James Grace is a lawyer, golf fanatic, and the author of *The Best Man's Handbook,* as well as the co-author of *The Art of Spooning*. Son of a lifelong golf lover, Jim held a golf club shortly after birth. He was an early master of miniature golf, and to this day he can perfectly time the windmill. He and his wife, Lisa, live in Boston, Massachusetts, with their two caddies-in-training, Avery and Cooper.

Brenda Brown is a freelance illustrator and cartoonist whose work has appeared in many books and major publications, including all the *The Worst-Case*

Scenario Survival Handbooks, *Reader's Digest*, the *Saturday Evening Post*, the *National Enquirer*, *Federal Lawyer*, and *National Review*. Her digital graphics have been incorporated into software programs developed by Adobe Systems, Deneba Software, Corel Corp, and many websites.

Check out www.worstcasescenarios.com for updates, new scenarios, and more! Because you just never know. . . .

More Worst-Case Scenarios

The Worst-Case Scenario Survival Handbook

The Worst-Case Scenario Survival Handbook: Travel

The Worst-Case Scenario Survival Handbook: Dating & Sex

The Worst-Case Scenario Survival Calendar

The Worst-Case Scenario Daily Survival Calendar

The Worst-Case Scenario Survival Journal

The Worst-Case Scenario Survival Cards: 30 Postcards

The Worst-Case Scenario Dating & Sex Address Book

*The Worst-Case Scenario Survival Handbook: Christmas
(Coming Fall 2002)*